RESUMES
FOR
COMPUTER
CAREERS

VGM Professional Resumes Series

RESUMES
FOR
COMPUTER
CAREERS

The Editors of
VGM Career Books

Second Edition, with Sample Cover Letters

VGM Career Books

Chicago   New York   San Francisco   Lisbon   London   Madrid   Mexico City
Milan   New Delhi   San Juan   Seoul   Singapore   Sydney   Toronto

Library of Congress Cataloging-in-Publication Data

Resumes for computer careers / the editors of VGM Career
Books. — 2nd ed., with sample cover letters.
      p.   cm. — (VGM professional resumes series)
    ISBN 0-07-138730-7
    1. Râsumâs (Employment).   2. Electronic data processing
personnel—Employment.   I. Series.
    HF5383 .R435   2002
    650.14'2—dc21   2002019978

VGM Career Books

A Division of The **McGraw·Hill** Companies

The editors gratefully acknowledge the assistance of Megan Phillips in the compiling and
editing of this book.

2 3 4 5 6 7 8 9 0 VLP VLP 0 5 4 3

ISBN 0-07-138730-7

This book was set in Minion by Ellen Kollmon
Printed and bound by Vicks Lithograph

This book is printed on acid-free paper.

Contents

Introduction

Your resume is a piece of paper (or an electronic document) that serves to introduce you to the people who will eventually hire you. To write a thoughtful resume, you must thoroughly assess your personality, your accomplishments, and the skills you have acquired. The act of composing and submitting a resume also requires you to carefully consider the company or individual that might hire you. What are they looking for, and how can you meet their needs? This book shows you how to organize your personal information and experience into a concise and well-written resume, so that your qualifications and potential as an employee will be understood easily and quickly by a complete stranger.

Writing the resume is just one step in what can be a daunting job-search process, but it is an important element in the chain of events that will lead you to your new position. While you are probably a talented, bright, and charming person, your resume may not reflect these qualities. A poorly written resume can get you nowhere; a well-written resume can land you an interview and potentially a job. A good resume can even lead the interviewer to ask you questions that will allow you to talk about your strengths and highlight the skills you can bring to a prospective employer. Even a person with very little experience can find a good job if he or she is assisted by a thoughtful and polished resume.

Lengthy, typewritten resumes are a thing of the past. Today, employers do not have the time or the patience for verbose documents; they look for tightly composed, straightforward, action-based resumes. Although a one-page resume is the norm, a two-page resume may be warranted if you have had extensive job experience or have changed careers and truly need the space to properly position yourself. If, after careful editing, you still need more than one page to present yourself, it's acceptable to use a second page. A crowded resume that's hard to read would be the worst of your choices.

Distilling your work experience, education, and interests into such a small space requires preparation and thought. This book takes you step-by-step through the process of crafting an effective resume that will stand out in today's competitive marketplace. It serves as a workbook and a place to write down your experiences, while also including the techniques you'll need to pull all the necessary elements together. In the following pages, you'll find many examples of resumes that are specific to your area of interest. Study them for inspiration and find what appeals to you. There are a variety of ways to organize and present your information; inside, you'll find several that will be suitable to your needs. Good luck landing the job of your dreams!

RESUMES
FOR
COMPUTER
CAREERS

The Elements of an Effective Resume

An effective resume is composed of information that employers are most interested in knowing about a prospective job applicant. This information is conveyed by a few essential elements. The following is a list of elements that are found in most resumes—some essential, some optional. Later in this chapter, we will further examine the role of each of these elements in the makeup of your resume.

- Heading
- Objective and/or Keyword Section
- Work Experience
- Education
- Honors
- Activities
- Certificates and Licenses
- Publications
- Professional Memberships
- Special Skills
- Personal Information
- References

The first step in preparing your resume is to gather information about yourself and your past accomplishments. Later you will refine this information, rewrite it using effective language, and organize it into an attractive layout. But first, let's take a look at each of these important elements individually so you can judge their appropriateness for your resume.

Heading

Although the heading may seem to be the simplest section of your resume, be careful not to take it lightly. It is the first section your prospective employer will see and it contains the information she or he will need to contact you. At the very least, the heading must contain your name, your home address, and, of course, a phone number where you can be reached easily.

In today's high-tech world, many of us have multiple ways that we can be contacted. You may list your E-mail address if you are reasonably sure the employer makes use of this form of communication. Keep in mind, however, that others may have access to your E-mail messages if you send them from an account provided by your current company. If this is a concern, do not list your work E-mail address on your resume. If you are able to take calls at your current place of business, you should include your work number, because most employers will attempt to contact you during typical business hours.

If you have voice mail or a reliable answering machine at home or at work, list its number in the heading and make sure your greeting is professional and clear. Always include at least one phone number in your heading, even if it is a temporary number, where a prospective employer can leave a message.

You might have a dozen different ways to be contacted, but you do not need to list all of them. Confine your numbers or addresses to those that are the easiest for the prospective employer to use and the simplest for you to retrieve.

Objective

When seeking a specific career path, it is important to list a job or career objective on your resume. This statement helps employers know the direction you see yourself taking, so they can determine whether your goals are in line with those of their organization and the position available. Normally, an objective is one to two sentences long. Its contents will vary depending on your career field, goals, and personality. The objective can be specific or general, but it should always be to the point. See the sample resumes in this book for examples.

If you are planning to use this resume online, or you suspect your potential employer is likely to scan your resume, you will want to include a "keyword" in the objective. This allows a prospective employer, searching hundreds of resumes for a specific skill or position objective, to locate the keyword and find your resume. In essence, a keyword is what's "hot" in your particular field at a given time. It's a buzzword, a shorthand way of getting a particular message across at a glance. For example, if you are a lawyer, your objective might state your desire to work in the area of corporate litigation. In this case, someone searching for the keyword "corporate litigation" will pull up your resume and know that you want to plan, research, and present cases at trial on behalf of the corporation. If your objective states that you "desire a challenging position in systems design," the keyword is "systems design," an industry-specific, shorthand way of saying that you want to be involved in assessing the need for, acquiring, and implementing high-technology systems. These are keywords and every industry has them, so it's becoming more and more important to include a few in your resume. (You may need to conduct additional research to make sure you know what keywords are most likely to be used in your desired industry, profession, or situation.)

There are many resume and job-search sites online. Like most things in the online world, they vary a great deal in quality. Use your discretion. If you plan to apply for jobs online or advertise your availability this way, you will want to design a scannable resume. This type of resume uses a format that can be easily scanned into a computer and added to a database. Scanning allows a prospective employer to use keywords to quickly review each applicant's experience and skills, and (in the event that there are many candidates for the job) to keep your resume for future reference.

Many people find that it is worthwhile to create two or more versions of their basic resume. You may want an intricately designed resume on high-quality paper to mail or hand out *and* a resume that is designed to be scanned into a computer and saved on a database or an online job site. You can even create a resume in ASCII text to E-mail to prospective employers. For further information, you may wish to refer to the *Guide to Internet Job Searching*, by Frances Roehm and Margaret Dikel, updated and published every other year by VGM Career Books, a division of the McGraw-Hill Companies. This excellent book contains helpful and detailed information about formatting a resume for Internet use. To get you started, in Chapter 3 we have included a list of things to keep in mind when creating electronic resumes.

Although it is usually a good idea to include an objective, in some cases this element is not necessary. The goal of the objective statement is to provide the employer with an idea of where you see yourself going in the field. However, if you are uncertain of the exact nature of the job you seek, including an objective that is too specific could result in your not being considered for a host of perfectly acceptable positions. If you decide not to use an objective heading in your resume, you should definitely incorporate the information that would be conveyed in the objective into your cover letter.

Work Experience

Work experience is arguably the most important element of them all. Unless you are a recent graduate with little or no relevant work experience, your current and former positions will provide the central focus of the resume. You will want this section to be as complete and carefully constructed as possible. By thoroughly examining your work experience, you can get to the heart of your accomplishments and present them in a way that demonstrates and highlights your qualifications.

If you are just out of school, your resume will probably focus on your education, but you should also include information on your work or volunteer experiences. Although you will have less information about work experience than a person who has held multiple positions or is advanced in his or her career, the amount of information is not what is most important in this section. How the information is presented and what it says about you as a worker and a person is what really counts.

As you create this section of your resume, remember the need for accuracy. Include all the necessary information about each of your jobs, including your job title, dates of employment, name of your employer, city, state, responsibilities, special projects you handled, and accomplishments. Be sure to list only accomplishments for which you were directly responsible. And don't be alarmed if you haven't participated in or worked on special projects, because this section may not be relevant to certain jobs.

The most common way to list your work experience is in *reverse chronological order*. In other words, start with your most recent job and work your way backward. This way, your prospective employer sees your current (and often most important) position before considering your past employment. Your most recent position, if it's the most important in terms of responsibilities and relevance to the job for which you are applying, should also be the one that includes the most information as compared to your previous positions.

If you are just out of school, highlight your summer employment, internships, and part-time work. As a recent graduate, however, you will probably begin your resume with your education section. The experience you gain with "starter jobs" in the workplace and your ability to juggle school and employment are important to most employers, even if the work itself seems unrelated to your proposed career path. If you were promoted or given greater responsibilities or commendations, be sure to mention the fact.

The following worksheet is provided to help you organize your experiences in the working world. It will also serve as an excellent resource to refer to when updating your resume in the future.

WORK EXPERIENCE

Job One:

Job Title _____

Dates _____

Employer _____

City, State _____

Major Duties _____

_____

_____

_____

_____

_____

_____

_____

_____

Special Projects _____

_____

_____

Accomplishments _____

_____

_____

_____

_____

_____

_____

Job Two:

Job Title _____

Dates _____

Employer _____

City, State _____

Major Duties _____

_____

_____

_____

_____

_____

_____

_____

_____

Special Projects _____

_____

_____

_____

Accomplishments _____

_____

_____

_____

_____

_____

_____

_____

_____

Job Three:

Job Title _____

Dates _____

Employer _____

City, State _____

Major Duties _____

_____

_____

_____

_____

_____

_____

_____

Special Projects _____

_____

_____

Accomplishments _____

_____

_____

_____

_____

_____

_____

Job Four:

Job Title _____

Dates _____

Employer _____

City, State _____

Major Duties _____

_____

_____

_____

_____

_____

_____

Special Projects _____

_____

_____

_____

Accomplishments _____

_____

_____

_____

_____

_____

_____

Education

Education is usually the second most important element of a resume. Your educational background is often a deciding factor in an employer's decision to interview you. Highlight your accomplishments in school as much as you did those accomplishments at work. If you are looking for your first professional job, your education will be your greatest asset because your related work experience will probably be minimal. In this case, the education section becomes the most important means of selling yourself.

Include in this section all the degrees or certificates you have received; your major or area of concentration; all of the honors you earned; and any relevant activities you participated in, organized, or chaired. Again, list your most recent schooling first. If you have completed graduate-level work, begin with that and work your way back through your undergraduate education. If you have completed college, you generally should not list your high school experience; do so only if you earned special honors, you had a grade point average that was much better than the norm, or this was your highest level of education.

If you have completed a large number of credit hours in a subject that may be relevant to the position you are seeking, but did not obtain a degree, you may wish to list the hours or classes you completed. Keep in mind, however, that you may be asked to explain why you did not finish the program. If you are currently in school, list the degree, certificate, or license you expect to obtain and the projected date of completion.

The following worksheet will help you gather the information you need for this section of your resume.

EDUCATION

School One _____

Major or Area of Concentration _____

Degree _____

Dates _____

School Two _____

Major or Area of Concentration _____

Degree _____

Dates _____

Honors

If you include an honors section in your resume, you should highlight any awards, honors, or memberships in honorary societies that you have received. (You may also incorporate this information into your education section.) Often, the honors are academic in nature, but this section also may be used for special achievements in sports, clubs, or other school activities. Always include the name of the organization awarding the honor and the date(s) received. Use the following worksheet to help you gather your information.

HONORS

Honor One _____

Awarding Organization _____

Date(s) _____

Honor Two _____

Awarding Organization _____

Date(s) _____

Honor Three _____

Awarding Organization _____

Date(s) _____

Honor Four _____

Awarding Organization _____

Date(s) _____

Honor Five _____

Awarding Organization _____

Date(s) _____

Activities

Perhaps you were active in different organizations or clubs during your years at school; often an employer will look at such involvement as evidence of initiative, dedication, and good social skills. Examples of your ability to take a leading role in a group should be included on a resume, if you can provide them. (Information about your activities also may be incorporated into your education section.) If you have been out of school for some time, the activities section of your resume can present neighborhood and community activities, volunteer positions, and so forth. In general, you may want to avoid listing any organization whose name indicates the race, creed, sex, age, marital status, sexual orientation, or nation of origin of its members because this could expose you to discrimination. Use the following worksheet to list the specifics of your activities.

ACTIVITIES

Organization/Activity _____

Accomplishments _____

_____

_____

Organization/Activity _____

Accomplishments _____

_____

_____

Organization/Activity _____

Accomplishments _____

_____

_____

As your work experience grows through the years, your school activities and honors will carry less weight and be emphasized less in your resume. Eventually, you will probably list only your degree and any major honors received. As time goes by, your job performance and the experience you've gained become the most important elements in your resume, which should change to reflect this.

Certificates and Licenses

If your chosen career path requires specialized training, you may already have certificates or licenses. You should list these if the job you are seeking requires them and you, of course, have acquired them. If you have applied for a license but have not yet received it, use the phrase "application pending."

License requirements vary by state. If you have moved or are planning to relocate to another state, check with that state's board or licensing agency for all licensing requirements.

Always make sure that all of the information you list is completely accurate. Locate copies of your certificates and licenses, and check the exact date and name of the accrediting agency. Use the following worksheet to organize the necessary information.

CERTIFICATES AND LICENSES

Name of License _____

Licensing Agency _____

Date Issued _____

Name of License _____

Licensing Agency _____

Date Issued _____

Name of License _____

Licensing Agency _____

Date Issued _____

Publications

Some professions strongly encourage or even require that you publish. If you have written, coauthored, or edited any books, articles, professional papers, or works of a similar nature that pertain to your field, you will definitely want to include this element. Remember to list the date of publication and the publisher's name, and specify whether you were the sole author or a coauthor. Book, magazine, or journal titles are generally italicized, while the titles of articles within a larger publication appear in quotes. (Check with your reference librarian for more about the appropriate way to present this information.) For scientific or research papers, you will need to give the date, place, and audience to whom the paper was presented.

Use the following worksheet to help you gather the necessary information about your publications.

PUBLICATIONS

Title and Type (Note, Article, etc.) _____

Title of Publication (Journal, Book, etc.) _____

Publisher _____

Date Published _____

Title and Type (Note, Article, etc.) _____

Title of Publication (Journal, Book, etc.) _____

Publisher _____

Date Published _____

Title and Type (Note, Article, etc.) _____

Title of Publication (Journal, Book, etc.) _____

Publisher _____

Date Published _____

Professional Memberships

Another potential element in your resume is a section listing professional memberships. Use this section to describe your involvement in professional associations, unions, and similar organizations. It is to your advantage to list any professional memberships that pertain to the job you are seeking. Many employers see your membership as representative of your desire to stay up-to-date and connected in your field. Include the dates of your involvement and whether you took part in any special activities or held any offices within the organization. Use the following worksheet to organize your information.

PROFESSIONAL MEMBERSHIPS

Name of Organization _____

Office(s) Held_____

Activities _____

Dates _____

Name of Organization _____

Office(s) Held_____

Activities _____

Dates _____

Name of Organization _____

Office(s) Held_____

Activities _____

Dates _____

Name of Organization _____

Office(s) Held_____

Activities _____

Dates _____

Special Skills

The special skills section of your resume is the place to mention any special abilities you have that relate to the job you are seeking. You can use this element to present certain talents or experiences that are not necessarily a part of your education or work experience. Common examples include fluency in a foreign language, extensive travel abroad, or knowledge of a particular computer application. "Special skills" can encompass a wide range of talents, and this section can be used creatively. However, for each skill you list, you should be able to describe how it would be a direct asset in the type of work you're seeking because employers may ask just that in an interview. If you can't think of a way to do this, it may be extraneous information.

Personal Information

Some people include personal information on their resumes. This is generally not recommended, but you might wish to include it if you think that something in your personal life, such as a hobby or talent, has some bearing on the position you are seeking. This type of information is often referred to at the beginning of an interview, when it may be used as an "icebreaker." Of course, personal information regarding your age, marital status, race, religion, or sexual orientation should never appear on your resume as *personal information*. It should be given only in the context of memberships and activities, and only when doing so would not expose you to discrimination.

References

References are not usually given on the resume itself, but a prospective employer needs to know that you have references who may be contacted if necessary. All you need to include is a single sentence at the end of the resume: "References are available upon request," or even simply, "References available." Have a reference list ready—your interviewer may ask to see it! Contact each person on the list ahead of time to see whether it is all right for you to use him or her as a reference. This way, the person has a chance to think about what to say *before* the call occurs. This helps ensure that you will obtain the best reference possible.

Chapter 2

Writing Your Resume

Now that you have gathered the information for each section of your resume, it's time to write it out in a way that will get the attention of the reviewer—hopefully, your future employer! The language you use in your resume will affect its success, so you must be careful and conscientious. Translate the facts you have gathered into the active, precise language of resume writing. You will be aiming for a resume that keeps the reader's interest and highlights your accomplishments in a concise and effective way.

Resume writing is unlike any other form of writing. Although your seventh-grade composition teacher would not approve, the rules of punctuation and sentence building are often completely ignored. Instead, you should try for a functional, direct writing style that focuses on the use of verbs and other words that imply action on your part. Writing with action words and strong verbs characterizes you to potential employers as an energetic, active person, someone who completes tasks and achieves results from his or her work. Resumes that do not make use of action words can sound passive and stale. These resumes are not effective and do not get the attention of any employer, no matter how qualified the applicant. Choose words that display your strengths and demonstrate your initiative. The following list of commonly used verbs will help you create a strong resume:

administered	assembled
advised	assumed responsibility
analyzed	billed
arranged	built

carried out	inspected
channeled	interviewed
collected	introduced
communicated	invented
compiled	maintained
completed	managed
conducted	met with
contacted	motivated
contracted	negotiated
coordinated	operated
counseled	orchestrated
created	ordered
cut	organized
designed	oversaw
determined	performed
developed	planned
directed	prepared
dispatched	presented
distributed	produced
documented	programmed
edited	published
established	purchased
expanded	recommended
functioned as	recorded
gathered	reduced
handled	referred
hired	represented
implemented	researched
improved	reviewed

saved	supervised
screened	taught
served as	tested
served on	trained
sold	typed
suggested	wrote

Let's look at two examples that differ only in their writing style. The first resume section is ineffective because it does not use action words to accent the applicant's work experiences:

WORK EXPERIENCE
Regional Sales Manager

Manager of sales representatives from seven states. Manager of twelve food chain accounts in the East. In charge of the sales force's planned selling toward specific goals. Supervisor and trainer of new sales representatives. Consulting for customers in the areas of inventory management and quality control.

Special Projects: Coordinator and sponsor of annual food industry sales seminar.

Accomplishments: Monthly regional volume went up 25 percent during my tenure while, at the same time, a proper sales/cost ratio was maintained. Customer-company relations were improved.

In the following paragraph, we have rewritten the same section using action words. Notice how the tone has changed. It now sounds stronger and more active. This person accomplished goals and really *did* things.

WORK EXPERIENCE
Regional Sales Manager

Managed sales representatives from seven states. Oversaw twelve food chain accounts in the eastern United States. Directed the sales force in planned selling toward specific goals. Supervised and trained new sales representatives. Counseled customers in the areas of inventory management and quality control. Coordinated and sponsored the annual Food Industry Seminar. Increased monthly regional volume 25 percent and helped to improve customer-company relations during my tenure.

One helpful way to construct the work experience section is to make use of your actual job descriptions—the written duties and expectations your employers had for a person in your current or former position. Job descriptions are rarely written in proper resume language, so you will have to rework them, but they do include much of the information necessary to create this section of your resume. If you have access to job descriptions for your former positions, you can use the details to construct an action-oriented paragraph. Often, your human resources department can provide a job description for your current position.

The following is an example of a typical human resources job description, followed by a rewritten version of the same description employing action words and specific details about the job. Again, pay attention to the style of writing instead of the content, as the details of your own experience will be unique.

WORK EXPERIENCE
Public Administrator I

Responsibilities: Coordinate and direct public services to meet the needs of the nation, state, or community. Analyze problems; work with special committees and public agencies; recommend solutions to governing bodies.

Aptitudes and Skills: Ability to relate to and communicate with people; solve complex problems through analysis; plan, organize, and implement policies and programs. Knowledge of political systems, financial management, personnel administration, program evaluation, and organizational theory.

WORK EXPERIENCE
Public Administrator I

Wrote pamphlets and conducted discussion groups to inform citizens of legislative processes and consumer issues. Organized and supervised 25 interviewers. Trained interviewers in effective communication skills.

After you have written out your resume, you are ready to begin the next important step: assembly and layout.

Chapter 3

Assembly and Layout

At this point, you've gathered all the necessary information for your resume and rewritten it in language that will impress your potential employers. Your next step is to assemble the sections in a logical order and lay them out on the page neatly and attractively to achieve the desired effect: getting the interview.

Assembly

The order of the elements in a resume makes a difference in its overall effect. Clearly, you would not want to bury your name and address somewhere in the middle of the resume. Nor would you want to lead with a less important section, such as special skills. Put the elements in an order that stresses your most important accomplishments and the things that will be most appealing to your potential employer. For example, if you recently graduated from school and have no full-time work experience, you will want the reviewer to read about your education before any part-time jobs you may have held during the vacations. On the other hand, if you have been gainfully employed for several years and currently hold an important position in your company, you should list your work accomplishments ahead of your educational information, which has become less pertinent with time.

Certain things should always be included in your resume, but others are optional. The following list shows you which are which. You might want to use it as a checklist to be certain that you have included all of the necessary information.

Essential	**Optional**
Name	Cellular Phone Number
Address	Pager Number
Phone Number	E-Mail Address or Website Address
Work Experience	Voice Mail Number
Education	Job Objective
References Phrase	Honors
	Special Skills
	Publications
	Professional Memberships
	Activities
	Certificates and Licenses
	Personal Information
	Graphics
	Photograph

Your choice of optional sections depends on your own background and employment needs. Always use information that will put you in a favorable light—unless it's absolutely essential, avoid anything that will prompt the interviewer to ask questions about your weaknesses or something else that could be unflattering. Make sure your information is accurate and truthful. If your honors are impressive, include them in the resume. If your activities in school demonstrate talents that are necessary for the job you are seeking, allow space for a section on activities. If you are applying for a position that requires ornamental illustration, you may want to include border illustrations or graphics that demonstrate your talents in this area. If you are answering an advertisement for a job that requires certain physical traits, a photo of yourself might be appropriate. A person applying for a job as a computer programmer would *not* include a photo as part of his or her resume. Each resume is unique, just as each person is unique.

Types of Resumes

So far we have focused on the most common type of resume—the *reverse chronological* resume—in which your most recent job is listed first. This is the type of resume usually preferred by those who have to read a large number of resumes, and it is by far the most popular and widely circulated. However, this style of presentation may not be the most effective way to highlight *your* skills and accomplishments.

For example, if you are reentering the workforce after many years or are trying to change career fields, the *functional* resume may work best. This type of resume puts the focus on your achievements instead of the sequence of your work history. In the functional resume, your experience is presented through your general accomplishments and the skills you have developed in your working life.

A functional resume is assembled from the same information you gathered in Chapter 1. The main difference lies in how you organize the information. Essentially, the work experience section is divided in two, with your job duties and accomplishments constituting one section and your employers' names, cities, and states; your positions; and the dates employed making up the other. Place the first section near the top of your resume, just below your job objective (if used), and call it *Accomplishments* or *Achievements*. The second section, containing the bare essentials of your work history, should come after the accomplishments section and can be called *Employment History*, since it is a chronological overview of your former jobs.

The other sections of your resume remain the same. The work experience section is the only one affected in the functional format. By placing the section that focuses on your achievements at the beginning, you draw attention to these achievements. This puts less emphasis on whom you worked for and when, and more on what you did and what you are capable of doing.

If you are changing careers, the emphasis on skills and achievements is important. The identities of previous employers (who aren't part of your new career field) need to be downplayed. A functional resume can help accomplish this task. If you are reentering the workforce after a long absence, a functional resume is the obvious choice. And if you lack full-time work experience, you will need to draw attention away from this fact and put the focus on your skills and abilities. You may need to highlight your volunteer activities and part-time work. Education may also play a more important role in your resume.

The type of resume that is right for you will depend on your personal circumstances. It may be helpful to create both types and then compare them. Which one presents you in the best light? Examples of both types of resumes are included in this book. Use the sample resumes in Chapter 5 to help you decide on the content, presentation, and look of your own resume.

Special Tips for Electronic Resumes

Because there are many details to consider in writing a resume that will be posted or transmitted on the Internet, or one that will be scanned into a computer when it is received, we suggest that you refer to the *Guide to Internet Job Searching*, by Frances Roehm and Margaret Dikel, as previously mentioned. However, here are some brief, general guidelines to follow if you expect your resume to be scanned into a computer.

- Use standard fonts in which none of the letters touch.

- Keep in mind that underlining, italics, and fancy scripts may not scan well.

- Use boldface and capitalization to set off elements. Again, make sure letters don't touch. Leave at least a quarter inch between lines of type.

- Keep information and elements at the left margin. Centering, columns, and even indenting may change when the resume is optically scanned.

- Do not use any lines, boxes, or graphics.

- Place the most important information at the top of the first page. If you use two pages, put "Page 1 of 2" at the bottom of the first page and put your name and "Page 2 of 2" at the top of the second page.

- List each telephone number on its own line in the header.

- Use multiple keywords or synonyms for what you do to make sure your qualifications will be picked up if a prospective employer is searching for them. Use nouns that are keywords for your profession.

- Be descriptive in your titles. For example, don't just use "assistant"; use "legal office assistant."

- Make sure the contrast between print and paper is good. Use a high-quality laser printer and white or very light-colored 8½-by-11-inch paper.

- Mail a high-quality laser print or an excellent copy. Do not fold or use staples, as this might interfere with scanning. You may, however, use paper clips.

In addition to creating a resume that works well for scanning, you may want to have a resume that can be E-mailed to reviewers. Because you may not know what word processing application the recipient uses, the best format to use is ASCII text. (ASCII stands for "American Standard Code for Information Exchange.") It allows people with very different software platforms to exchange and understand information. (E-mail operates on this principle.) ASCII is a simple, text-only language, which means you can include only simple text. There can be no use of boldface, italics, or even paragraph indentations.

To create an ASCII resume, just use your normal word processing program; when finished, save it as a "text only" document. You will find this option under the "save" or "save as" command. Here is a list of things to *avoid* when crafting your electronic resume:

- Tabs. Use your space bar. Tabs will not work.

- Any special characters, such as mathematical symbols.

- Word wrap. Use hard returns (the return key) to make line breaks.

- Centering or other formatting. Align everything at the left margin.

- Bold or italic fonts. Everything will be converted to plain text when you save the file as a "text only" document.

Check carefully for any mistakes before you save the document as a text file. Spellcheck and proofread it several times, then ask someone with a keen eye to go over it again for you. Remember: the key is to keep it simple. Any attempt to make this resume pretty or decorative may result in a resume that is confusing and hard to read. After you have saved the document, you can cut and paste it into an E-mail or onto a website.

Layout for a Paper Resume

A great deal of care—and much more formatting—is necessary to achieve an attractive layout for your paper resume. There is no single appropriate layout that applies to every resume, but there are a few basic rules to follow in putting your resume on paper:

- Leave a comfortable margin on the sides, top, and bottom of the page (usually one to one and a half inches).

- Use appropriate spacing between the sections (two to three line spaces are usually adequate).

- Be consistent in the *type* of headings you use for different sections of your resume. For example, if you capitalize the heading EMPLOY-MENT HISTORY, don't use initial capitals and underlining for a section of equal importance, such as <u>Education</u>.

- Do not use more than one font in your resume. Stay consistent by choosing a font that is fairly standard and easy to read, and don't change it for different sections. Beware of the tendency to try to make your resume original by choosing fancy type styles; your resume may end up looking unprofessional instead of creative. Unless you are in a very creative and artistic field, you should almost always stick with tried-and-true type styles like Times New Roman and Palatino, which are often used in business writing. In the area of resume styles, conservative is usually the best way to go.

- Always try to fit your resume on one page. If you are having trouble with this, you may be trying to say too much. Edit out any repetitive or unnecessary information, and shorten descriptions of earlier jobs where possible. Ask a friend you trust for feedback on what seems unnecessary or unimportant. For example, you may have included too many optional sections. Today, with the prevalence of the personal computer as a tool, there is no excuse for a poorly laid-out resume. Experiment with variations until you are pleased with the result.

CHRONOLOGICAL RESUME

Lucas Jackson
2399 S. Division • Grand Rapids, MI 49503
(616) 555-9354
Cell: (616) 555-2819
lucasjackson@xxx.com

Objective

Apply my skills as a content expert to a new challenge with a company focused on quality, dedication, and ingenuity.

Work

1998 to present

Content Strategist, Sonic Consulting, Grand Rapids, MI

Provide digital solutions for clients interested in establishing their presence online. Make recommendations on content assets, third-party content partnerships, and content management systems. Direct copywriters and design teams to fulfill the clients' objectives and create brand strategies.

1996 to 1998

Website Manager, *Crash! Magazine*, Detroit, MI

Directed the online version of *Crash! Magazine* and ensured design and content guidelines of the site followed those of the print version. Coordinated special events to drive traffic to the site resulting in a 75 percent increase in hits over four months. Created and edited content specifically for the site to establish its own identity.

1994 to 1996

Writer, *Digital City Magazine*, Detroit, MI

Researched and wrote articles covering the emerging Internet business and issues that relate to that unique business sector. Interviewed people involved in cutting-edge development on the Web and analyzed the business implications of this unique medium.

Skills

- Intimate familiarity with standard style guides including *AP, Chicago Manual, MLA,* and *Wired.*
- Very knowledgeable in the use and merits of content management systems such as Vignette, ePrise, and BroadVision.
- Uncanny ability to merge creative vision with business objectives to create distinctive and engaging content.

References available upon request

FUNCTIONAL RESUME

Katrina Parker
1402 Greenbriar Road
Charleston, WV 25304
(304) 555-1704

Applications & Systems Programmer

Credentials

- B.S. in Computer Science—March 1995—University of Michigan; minor in Accounting
- Knowledge of COBOL, FORTRAN, Pascal, C, C Plus, BASIC, CAD/CAM, RPG II, ASSEMBLY language #68000, 8086 & 6502, and dbase
- High level of self-motivation and attention to detail

Job Duties

- Code, test, debug, and maintain programs
- Create program documentation
- Integrate new hardware into existing systems
- Diagnose and correct systems failures
- Maintain monitors, database packages, compilers, assemblers, and utility programs
- Select and modify new hardware and software to company specifications

Achievements

- Designed programs in C Plus for Heritage Bank to coordinate functions of ATM machines
- Purchased new hardware and software for Advantage Publishers, modified equipment to suit company's needs and resolve interoperability issues

Employers

Heritage Bank	6/99 to Present
Advantage Publishers	4/96 to 6/99

References

Marta Dalton	Renu Das
Vice President of Finance	Director of Human Resources
Heritage Bank	Advantage Publishers
411 Watkins Street	694 Dale Street
Charleston, WV 25304	Deer Park, NY 11729
(304) 555-2225, Ext. 203	(516) 555-7937

Remember that a resume is not an autobiography. Too much information will only get in the way. The more compact your resume, the easier it will be to review. If a person who is swamped with resumes looks at yours, catches the main points, and then calls you for an interview to fill in some of the details, your resume has already accomplished its task. A clear and concise resume makes for a happy reader and a good impression.

There are times when, despite extensive editing, the resume simply cannot fit on one page. In this case, the resume should be laid out on two pages in such a way that neither clarity nor appearance is compromised. Each page of a two-page resume should be marked clearly: the first should indicate "Page 1 of 2," and the second should include your name and the page number, for example, "Julia Ramirez—Page 2 of 2." The pages should then be stapled together. You may use a smaller font (in the same font as the body of your resume) for the page numbers. Place them at the bottom of page one and the top of page two. Again, spend the time now to experiment with the layout until you find one that looks good to you.

Always show your final layout to other people and ask them what they like or dislike about it, and what impresses them most when they read your resume. Make sure that their responses are the same as what you want to elicit from your prospective employer. If they aren't the same, you should continue to make changes until the necessary information is emphasized.

Proofreading

After you have finished typing the master copy of your resume and before you have it copied or printed, thoroughly check it for typing and spelling errors. Do not place all your trust in your computer's spellcheck function. Use an old editing trick and read the whole resume backward—start at the end and read it right to left and bottom to top. This can help you see the small errors or inconsistencies that are easy to overlook. Take time to do it right because a single error on a document this important can cause the reader to judge your attention to detail in a harsh light.

Have several people look at the finished resume just in case you've missed an error. Don't try to take a shortcut; not having an unbiased set of eyes examine your resume now could mean embarrassment later. Even experienced editors can easily overlook their own errors. Be thorough and conscientious with your proofreading so your first impression is a perfect one.

We have included the following rules of capitalization and punctuation to assist you in the final stage of creating your resume. Remember that resumes often require use of a shorthand style of writing that may include sentences without periods and other stylistic choices that break the standard rules of grammar. Be consistent in each section, and throughout the whole resume, with your choices.

RULES OF CAPITALIZATION

- Capitalize proper nouns, such as names of schools, colleges, and universities; names of companies; and brand names of products.

- Capitalize major words in the names and titles of books, tests, and articles that appear in the body of your resume.

- Capitalize words in major section headings of your resume.

- Do not capitalize words just because they seem important.

- When in doubt, consult a manual of style such as *Words into Type* (Prentice-Hall) or *The Chicago Manual of Style* (The University of Chicago Press). Your local library can help you locate these and other reference books. Many computer programs also have grammar help sections.

RULES OF PUNCTUATION

- Use commas to separate words in a series.

- Use a semicolon to separate series of words that already include commas within the series. (For an example, see the first rule of capitalization.)

- Use a semicolon to separate independent clauses that are not joined by a conjunction.

- Use a period to end a sentence.

- Use a colon to show that examples or details follow that will expand or amplify the preceding phrase.

- Avoid the use of dashes.

- Avoid the use of brackets.

- If you use any punctuation in an unusual way in your resume, be consistent in its use.

- Whenever you are uncertain, consult a style manual.

Putting Your Resume in Print

You will need to buy high-quality paper for your printer before you print your finished resume. Regular office paper is not good enough for resumes; the reviewer will probably think it looks flimsy and cheap. Go to an office supply store or copy shop and select a high-quality bond paper that will make a good first impression. Select colors like white, off-white, or possibly a light gray. In some industries, a pastel may be acceptable, but be sure the color and feel of the paper makes a subtle, positive statement about you. Nothing in the choice of paper should be loud or unprofessional.

If your computer printer does not reproduce your resume properly and produces smudged or stuttered type, either ask to borrow a friend's or take your disk (or a clean original) to a printer or copy shop for high-quality copying. If you anticipate needing a large number of copies, taking your resume to a copy shop or a printer is probably the best choice.

Hold a sheet of your unprinted bond paper up to the light. If it has a watermark, you will want to point this out to the person helping you with copies; the printing should be done so that the reader can read the print and see the watermark the right way up. Check each copy for smudges or streaks. This is the time to be a perfectionist—the results of your careful preparation will be well worth it.

Chapter 4

The Cover Letter

Once your resume has been assembled, laid out, and printed to your satisfaction, the next and final step before distribution is to write your cover letter. Though there may be instances where you deliver your resume in person, you will usually send it through the mail or online. Resumes sent through the mail always need an accompanying letter that briefly introduces you and your resume. The purpose of the cover letter is to get a potential employer to read your resume, just as the purpose of the resume is to get that same potential employer to call you for an interview.

Like your resume, your cover letter should be clean, neat, and direct. A cover letter usually includes the following information:

1. Your name and address (unless it already appears on your personal letterhead) and your phone number(s); see item 7.

2. The date.

3. The name and address of the person and company to whom you are sending your resume.

4. The salutation ("Dear Mr." or "Dear Ms." followed by the person's last name, or "To Whom It May Concern" if you are answering a blind ad).

5. An opening paragraph explaining why you are writing (for example, in response to an ad, as a follow-up to a previous meeting, at the suggestion of someone you both know) and indicating that you are interested in whatever job is being offered.

6. One or more paragraphs that tell why you want to work for the company and what qualifications and experiences you can bring to the position. This is a good place to mention some detail about

that particular company that makes you want to work for them; this shows that you have done some research before applying.

7. A final paragraph that closes the letter and invites the reviewer to contact you for an interview. This can be a good place to tell the potential employer which method would be best to use when contacting you. Be sure to give the correct phone number and a good time to reach you, if that is important. You may mention here that your references are available upon request.

8. The closing ("Sincerely" or "Yours truly") followed by your signature in a dark ink, with your name typed under it.

Your cover letter should include all of this information and be no longer than one page in length. The language used should be polite, businesslike, and to the point. Don't attempt to tell your life story in the cover letter; a long and cluttered letter will serve only to annoy the reader. Remember that you need to mention only a few of your accomplishments and skills in the cover letter. The rest of your information is available in your resume. If your cover letter is a success, your resume will be read and all pertinent information reviewed by your prospective employer.

Producing the Cover Letter

Cover letters should always be individualized because they are always written to specific individuals and companies. Never use a form letter for your cover letter or copy it as you would a resume. Each cover letter should be unique, and as personal and lively as possible. (Of course, once you have written and rewritten your first cover letter until you are satisfied with it, you can certainly use similar wording in subsequent letters. You may want to save a template on your computer for future reference.) Keep a hard copy of each cover letter so you know exactly what you wrote in each one.

There are sample cover letters in Chapter 6. Use them as models or for ideas of how to assemble and lay out your own cover letters. Remember that every letter is unique and depends on the particular circumstances of the individual writing it and the job for which he or she is applying.

After you have written your cover letter, proofread it as thoroughly as you did your resume. Again, spelling or punctuation errors are a sure sign of carelessness, and you don't want that to be a part of your first impression on a prospective employer. This is no time to trust your spellcheck function. Even after going through a spelling and grammar check, your cover letter should be carefully proofread by at least one other person.

Print the cover letter on the same quality bond paper you used for your resume. Remember to sign it, using a good, dark-ink pen. Handle the letter and resume carefully to avoid smudging or wrinkling, and mail them together in an appropriately sized envelope. Many stores sell matching envelopes to coordinate with your choice of bond paper.

Keep an accurate record of all resumes you send out and the results of each mailing. This record can be kept on your computer, in a calendar or notebook, or on file cards. Knowing when a resume is likely to have been received will keep you on track as you make follow-up phone calls.

About a week after mailing resumes and cover letters to potential employers, contact them by telephone. Confirm that your resume arrived and ask whether an interview might be possible. Be sure to record the name of the person you spoke to and any other information you gleaned from the conversation. It is wise to treat the person answering the phone with a great deal of respect; sometimes the assistant or receptionist has the ear of the person doing the hiring.

You should make a great impression with the strong, straightforward resume and personalized cover letter you have just created. We wish you every success in securing the career of your dreams!

Chapter 5

Sample Resumes

This chapter contains dozens of sample resumes for people pursuing a wide variety of jobs and careers in the field of information services, or who have had experience in this field in the past.

There are many different styles of resumes in terms of layout and presentation of information. These samples also represent people with varying amounts of education and work experience. Model your resume after these samples. Choose one resume or borrow elements from several different resumes to help you construct your own.

CATHY SMITH
546 Elm Street
Chicago, IL 60645
312-555-3894
cathysmith@xxx.com

GOAL

Computer science professional with experience in customer service and technical writing seeks customer service position with potential for supervisory responsibility.

WORK HISTORY

2-96 to Present:
Technical Writer
Superior Software Products, Chicago, IL

Prepare technical manuals for end users of Superior Software Products. Obtain program feature specifications from programmers and systems engineers to develop step-by-step instructions, written in clear, nontechnical language. Supervise ongoing revision and updating of manuals. Implement and test user experience guidelines to ensure directions are understood. Product line includes desktop publishing, graphic arts, word processing, and database products.

4-92 to 2-96:
Customer Service Technician
Worthington Software, Palatine, IL

Served as customer support contact for end users of Worthington Software and as telephone troubleshooter for clients, providing step-by-step solutions for online difficulties. Maintained phone log of customer problems. Worked with systems engineers and technical writers to modify systems designs and revise instructional manuals as necessary.

EDUCATION

University of Illinois at Chicago
Computer Career Training Program, One-year Graduate Certificate, completed 1-96

Northern Illinois University
B.S. Degree, completed 1-95

References Available

Malik Van
2500 Central Street
Drake's Bay, Florida 33001
409/555-6789
Cell: 409/555/8776
mvanman@xxx.com

Objective:
To procure a software engineering position with potential for advancement.

Experience:
1997 - present
Northside Computer Access, Senior Systems Designer
Develop I/0 interfaces and create/support file transfer systems. Extensive use of IBM 370, Cyber 175, VAX-11/780 and IBM VM/CMS.

1993 - 1997
King Software, Technical Advisor
Provided marketing and sales support for extensive software product lines including, spreadsheets, word processing programs, graphics, and database applications.

1991 - 1993
Brides & Franklin Development, Senior Programmer
Team leader for software development group. Promoted from programmer to senior programmer after one year.

Credentials:
M.I.S. Florida Technical Institute, 1993
B.S. Iowa State University, 1985

DEC VAX 11/780, Intel Software, C, C+, Unix Systems, MS/DOS, VMS, Pascal, BASIC, Kermit, PC-BitCom, PC-ProCom, relational model CODASYL, and database implementation on SQL/DS and IDMS/DBTG DBMS.

References:
Available upon request.

Martin K. Meade
411 West Street • (617) 555-6786 Home • (617) 555-5600 Work • Boston, MA 02129

Skills
IMS/DB & DC, CICS and DB2 using COBOL, RAMIS, IFPS, EASYTRIEVE, EASYTRIEVE Plus, and TELON. IBM8100/DPPX, Prime 750, Honeywell GCOS6.

Professional Experience
Eleven years systems experience in IBM operating systems, IBM machines, and IBM PC/LAN workstations. Extensive use of Standard TAPS Code and converted TAPS on IBM8100/DPPX. A proven record of delivering computerized systems under tight deadlines to meet exacting requirements.

Taylor Healthcare Corporation   1989 - Present
Senior Programmer Analyst   1994 - Present
- Lead a team of seven analysts in installing the INFOPAC report distribution system, which reduced Freight printed output by 85 percent. Responsible for work plans, headcount utilization, program specifications, and user training
- Developed software to interface with IFPS (Interactive Financial Planning System) and ran graph system
- Convert all CICS programs from one system to another, updating JCL and complying with new systems standards
- Provide application support of the Freight/DCMS (Distribution Center Management System)

Programmer Analyst   1990-1994
- Converted interface to general ledger system from MSA to M & D. Created all necessary program specifications
- Developed program specifications, trained APAs and Co-op students, produced programs necessary for marketing of the Dealer Business System to an external division
- Designed, implemented, and supported additional Dealer Business Subsystems using CICS, VSAM, TELON, COBOL, EASYTRIEVE, and EASYTRIEVE Plus

Associate Programmer Analyst   1989-1990
- Provided user interface for METAPHOR system. Designed databases, managed query processing using SQL, and provided all necessary user training
- Completed training in IMS DB/DC, VSAM, and DB/DC BAL
- Completed continuing education course in COBOL programming and Method One structured methodology techniques

Education
A.A. in Computer Studies
Boston Junior College, graduated 1989

B.T. in Technical Writing
Massachusetts Institute of Technology, graduated 1991

References Available

Angela Goosen

9324 N. Elm St.
Dallas, TX 75270
(214) 555-2223
angelagoosen@xxx.com

Background

Twelve years of system design and maintenance. Proven track record as supervisor of junior staff. Dedicated professional focused on quality and reliability.

Education

B.S. Information Technology, University of Texas, 1988

Employment

Cannon Corp., Ft. Worth, TX (June 1996 to Present)
Supervisor
Upgraded and expanded computer network system. Reported directly to vice president of operations. Designed and implemented inventory control system. Participated in market development program. Supervised and guided ten junior staff members and ensured systems operated consistently at peak performance.

Sweetwater Systems, Dallas, TX (April 1993 to June 1996)
Senior System Designer
Wrote database for electronic key systems. Trained telephone end users to use on-screen order-taking program. Developed computer-assisted learning program to train new staff. Supervised eight employees.

Mead & Johnson, LLC, Dallas, TX (May 1988 to April 1993)
System Analyst
Maintained networks. Installed upgraded software and hardware. Promoted to Lead Analyst after two years.

References available upon request

BARBARA ZABRISKIE

655 COOK ROAD
ORMOND BEACH, FL 32176
(904) 555-4968 HOME
(904) 555-2078 WORK
EMAIL: BARBZ@XXX.COM

• OVERVIEW •

More than a decade in data processing, with past four years spent in DB2 and CICS analysis, design, and development. Proven ability to utilize extensive knowledge of information systems.

• ACHIEVEMENTS •

- Designed SQL statements for heavy report requests. Tested and executed SQL statements for proper syntax, logic, and execution.

- Experienced in development, new specification writing, modification, logical and physical design, structural procedures testing, and various financial applications using COBOL, DB2, CICS, and VSAM.

- Improved, expanded, and adapted Order Processing System consisting of 152 DB2 tables and views, BSAM files, and more than 100 online and batch programs.

- Designed new DB2 application called Order Tracking. Created four new tables and merged them with existing tables from original database.

• TECHNICAL EXPERTISE •

Languages: COBOL, BAL, FORTRAN, BASIC, and SQL

Operating Systems: MVS/ESA, MVS/JCL, DOS/VS/VSE, MS DOS

Software: VSAM, CICS, DB2, INS DB, TSO/SPF/ISPF, PARADOX 4.5, WINDOWS, QUATTRO PRO 5, EASE, QMF, MVS-ESA, DYNAM-D, Lotus, Pascal

Hardware: IBM 3090, 4381, PS/2, 8100/9370, IBM PC compatibles, SYSTEM 38

Page 1 of 2

• EDUCATION •

B.S. Computer Science University of Florida, 1992

Washington Technical Institute, 1994 - 1996
Courses:
- DB2 Fundamentals and Application Analysis
- Professional Systems Analysis
- CICS Program
- System Analysis and Design for Data Processing
- COBOL, FORTRAN, ASSEMBLER, and BASIC Programming and more

• EMPLOYERS •

***Consultant*, Warren Manufacturing, 10/97 - Present**
Ormond Beach, Florida

***System Analyst*, Horton Financial Managers, Inc., 9/94 - 10/97**
Key West, Florida

***Programmer Analyst*, PCX Industries, 8/92 - 9/94**
Richmond, Virginia

• REFERENCES •

Personal and professional references will be forwarded upon request.

Beverly Jackson

1800 West Sheridan Avenue • Atlanta, Georgia 30356
(770) 555-6978 Work • (770) 555-5836 Home
beverlyjackson@xxx.com

Goal
Systems Analysis and Programming Projects

Experience
Independent Contractor from 8/91 to Present

Recent Projects:
University of Georgia, Programming Consultant
Two-month project testing and executing SQL statements in QMF, SPUFI, or CANDLE EXPLAIN. Fine-tuned statements for efficient execution by the Optimize, using QMF or CANDLE EXPLAIN. Wrote all programs and all specifications for batch processing.

New World Packaging Inc., Independent Systems Analyst
One-year contract. Responsibilities included development, specifications writing, modification of existing programs as necessary, and design and coding of new programs. Performed structural procedure testing. Responsible for data and program modifications, recompiling and rebinding, testing and debugging.

Georgia Chemical Corporation, Independent Programmer
Assisted with set up of 30-member data processing department in Georgia branch office. Assignment included analyzing, coding, debugging, and implementing business applications, including payroll, general ledger, and inventory control. Implemented scientific applications such as process modeling and engineering. Performed troubleshooting. Expanded and interconnected system hardware.

Technical Knowledge

Languages	Systems	Software
COBOL	MVS/JCL	VSAM
COBOL II	MVS/ESA	IBM DB
FORTRAN	EASYTRIEVE	CICS
SQL	DOS/VS/VSE	DB2
BAL	MS DOS	QUICKEN
BASIC		EASE

Education
B.S. in Computer Science, Roosevelt University, 1991

References
Available on Request

Shari Suvari

2234 Ashland Blvd.
Bradenton, FL. 34203
941-555-8877
suvari123@xxx.com

Career Objective

Seeking an entry-level position as a programmer with established company willing to utilize my data processing experience.

Education

University of Florida, Bachelor of Science, May 2001
Major: Computer Science

Professional Experience

September 2001 to present
Macro Computer Sciences Institute, Tampa, FL

Junior Programmer
Member of data conversion team that converted UNISYS environment to IBM for a COBOL/CICS application system.

April 1999 to September 2001
University of Florida Computer Lab, Tampa, FL

Assisted students with various computer-related issues including rebooting, formatting disks, and creating databases. Also oversaw assignment of computers to students and helped troubleshoot any difficulties inexperienced users engaged.

References

Bob Arnold
Owner, Macro Computer Institute
941-555-8885
bobarnold@xxx.com

Liam OíNeal
Student Supervisor, U of F Computer Lab
941-555-3215
oneal223@xxx.com

RESUME
OF
KEVIN SCHULTZ
Consultant
1302 Willow Road • Oak Brook, IL 60521 • (708) 555-5732
(708) 555-5733 - Fax • kevs@xxx.com

OVERVIEW

Kevin Schultz has more than twenty years of technical experience in a wide variety of industries, including finance, manufacturing, insurance, and health care. He has extensive skill in database and online applications, design through implementation; system conversions; and multilanguage with both mainframes and PCs.

HARDWARE

IBM Mainframe	Honeywell	IBM PC
NCR	PC/XT/AT	SYSTEM 38

SOFTWARE

COBOL	APS	BAL
COBOL II	C	EASYTRIEVE PLUS
FILE-AID	FORTRAN	M BASIC
NEAT 3	UFO	PASCAL
PL/1	RPG II	CICS MACR0
CICS COMMAND	ADABAS	DB2
DBASE II	DM	DMS
IDMS	NOMAD II	TOTAL
CPM	GCOS	DOS/JCL
DOS/VS	DOS/VSE	OS
OS/MVS	OS/MV/XA	MS/DOS
PC/DOS	UIVAC-EXEC 8	JES 2
JES 3	BDAM	ISAM
VSAM	CLIST	CMS
ROSCOE	TSO	EXEC
ISPF	LIBRARIAN	PANVALET
XEDIT	ETHERNET	BASIC

RECENT CLIENTS

Adventure Outfitters

Improved order preparation for this mail order retailer. Batch environment using DB/2 and written in COBOL was used to reduce repetitive updates to DB/2 tables by perfecting all information to be updated, then processing the information in sequential files. After updating the data, the DB/2 tables were updated with the new information.

Premier Healthcare Systems

Extended internal online system-wide CICS macro facility, using BAL. Developed drug locker inventory control and reorder subsystem. Developed an online outpatient accounting system using CICS command and COBOL. Created online group accident and health claim processing system in CICS macro and COBOL.

EDUCATION

B.S. Computer Science
Southern Illinois University

REFERENCES

Available upon request

RP On-Line Inc.

Randy Paterniti
372 Ashurst Road
Boulder, CO 80321
(303) 555-5121 Work
rponline@xxx.com

Hardware

IBM 039X, 308X, 43XX, 50XX, IBM PC/XT/AT,
MACINTOSH

Software

DB2, TERADATA, IMS/DB, MVS/XA, CICS, APS, SQL/DS, QMF, TSO/ISPF, VM/CMS,
SYNCSORT, PLATINUM, MS WINDOWS, SYMPHONY, PANVALET, FOCUS,
IDCAMS, VSAM, ICCF, and special MSDOS

Languages

COBOL, COBOL II, Adabas, CICS, Relia, PL/1, JCL, REXX, EXEC,
EXEC 2, GPSS

Work Experience

Owner, RP On-Line Inc., 6/94 to Present

Sitka Pharmaceuticals. Responsible for major data conversion effort. Data converted from Unisys and Texas Instruments computer environments into DB2. Actively involved in all phases of application development from design through coding and testing to implementation. Conversion interfaces written in COBOL II, DB2.

Colorado Commercial Bank.   Converted billing system from IMS to DB2. Programs were written in COBOL with embedded SQL, CICS, and DB2. Actively involved in design of the new front-end for the same system, using PowerBuilder.

ABC Stores.   Member of the consumer marketing database team.
Responsible for analysis; relational database design; specifications; coding, testing, and implementation of the retail marketing information system, optimizing SQL code. Coding was done in APS, SQL, and DB2.

Woodruff Financial Services.   Performed enhancements of the existing applications processing system. Programs were written in PL/1.

Education

Computer Technologies Inc.
1996 Windows OS Certificate
1994 Sybase/Microsoft SQL Server Programming and Design
1993 PowerBuilder Application Development

University of Colorado
1992 M.S. in Computer Science
1990 B.S. in Computer Science

References Available

DAVIS P. ROBINSON

3988 Wagner Road
Cottonwood, CA 960223
(916) 555-6333

TECHNICAL SKILLS

Hardware: IBM 3090, 3081, IBM PS2-PC
Software: COBOL, COBOL II, SQL, BAL
Environments: MVS, MVS/XA, MVS/ESA
Communications: IMS/DC, CICS, DIALOG MANAGER
Databases: DB2, IMS/DLI, VSAM
Code Generators: TELON, APS
Analysis: YOUDON, OBJECT-ORIENTED
Applications:

Order Entry	Procurement	Distribution	Retailing
Personnel	Inventory	Warehousing	MRP
Purchasing	Training	Billing	Accounting

EDUCATION

M.S. Computer Technology, University of Southern California
B.S. Business, Washington State University

CONSULTING EXPERIENCE

Pacific Agribusiness Inc. - 1 year - CICS/TELON/VMS
Responsibilities: Systems Analysis, Design, and Code

Created plant maintenance system, which includes purchasing, inventory control, accounting, and other manufacturing systems.

The State of California - 8 months - IMS/TELON/VSAM
Responsibilities: System Analysis, Design, and Code

Rewrote the state's Medicare and Medicaid hospital claims system, in order to comply with new U.S. government regulations.

California Bell - 1 year - DB2/C/CS/IMS/TELON
Responsibilities: System Analysis, Detail Design, and Code

Developed a telephone service order entry system used to provide state-of-the-art technical service.

Page 1 of 2

American Academy of Nutrition - 5 months - DB2/C/CSITELON
Responsibilities: System Analysis, Detail Design, and Code

Developed marketing executive bonus incentive system. Online system was used to calculate and report on upper management's monetary incentives.

TechnoTemps - 1.5 years - DB2/C/CSITELON
Responsibilities: System Analysis, Definition, Design, and Code

Replaced an old batch IMS system with an online DB2 system. The application was a commercial finance system for one of TechnoTemp's clients.

Katzen Electron - 5 months - DB2/CICS/IMS/TELON
Responsibilities: System Analysis, Definition, and Design

Redesigned an old batch IMS system into an online interactive system. The application was a corporate procurement system used to assign worldwide contracts to Katzen vendors.

GT Telecommunications - 1 year - DB2/CICS/DIALOG MANAGER/APS
Responsibilities: System Analysis, User Contact, Design, and Code

Worked in employee training developing an employee class attendance and registration system.

Garden Foods - 6 months - IMS/DB/DC
Responsibilities: System Analysis, Design, and Code

Project development of a new centralized distribution and warehousing system.

Stevens Electronics - 1.3 years - IMS/DB/DC
Responsibilities: System Engineering, System Analysis

PAC III was our project management tool. Participated in MRP II training and education as well as working to make existing programs compatible with MRP II databases. Interfaced with many middle and upper management users, administrators, and other user contacts.

References on Request

Karen Feldman

877 Chesterfield Street • Lincolnwood, IL 60646 • (708) 555-9113
Cell: (708) 555-7768 • karenfeldman@xxx.com

Overview
Experienced systems programmer with background in consumer goods, telecommunications, and automotive industries.

Technical Knowledge
COBOL II, IMS/DB, DBS, SQL, DB2, TERADATA, TESSERACT, CICS, FOCUS, SYMPHONY, PARADOX, VM/CMS, QMF, IMS, DB/DC, VSAM, IMS/DB-DC

Work Record
- Consultant to following companies 1993 - Present
  - New Age Organic Foods, Inc.
  - American Telecommunications Inc.
  - Drexler Automotive Systems
  - Southern Telecommunications Systems

Achievements

New Age Organic Foods
- Successfully implemented new DataScan system for sales and marketing user group. System processed and converted information provided by Consumer Information Inc. and loaded it into TERADATA and DB2.
- Created new salary planning system using TESSERACT personnel management system in DB2 and CICS. Wrote programs in COBOL II, CICS, with embedded SQL.
- Converted accounts receivable system into MSA format. Wrote interfaces in COBOL under MVS/XA.

American Telecommunications Inc.
- Developed new billing system based on DB2.
- Developed production applications using COBOL, CICS, and embedded SQL.
- Created ad-hoc reports using QMF and SQL.

Drexler Automotive Systems
- Timely and competently completed inventory, order entry, and conversion projects.
- Successfully completed supervisor training program.
- Serviced as Assistant Quality Control Supervisor.
- Successfully supervised online inspectors, under direction of Quality Control Supervisor.

Southern Telecommunications Systems
- Successfully developed fixed assets systems for newly formed corporate division.
- Created online manufacturing tracking and inventory control system.
- Designed and implemented new telephone invoicing system incorporating PC to mainframe interaction.

Education
B.S. Computer Science, Northern Illinois University - 1993

References
Personal and professional references available and forwarded upon request.

Jack Anderson

3646 N. Damen
Chicago, IL 60625
(773) 555-7293
jackanderson@xxx.com

Content Management Specialist

Education

B.A. English, University of Chicago
M.F.A. University of Chicago

Professional Development

Presently the Content Manager for Alysis Systems, Chicago. Create original content for specialty sites devoted to promoting international brands. Research, write, and edit online articles for these sites and ensure all content meets stringent style outlines and standards.

From 1995 until 1998, Writer for *Internet News Daily*. Along with creating articles, I acted as managing editor for staff writers and freelancers ensuring my department met daily deadlines and upheld the highest journalistic standards. Populated content for three sections of the site and helped develop promotional campaigns.

My career started as a copywriter for Travis Toys where from 1992 to 1995 I wrote product descriptions and news releases for one of America's most beloved and recognized companies. I worked extensively with product managers to develop copy that conveyed the feeling of the company to children and adults alike.

References

Clarke Roberts, Editor
Internet News Daily
(312) 555-3332
clarkeroberts@xxx.com

Matt Schuba, Marketing Manager
Travis Toys
(312) 555-0033
mattschuba@xxx.com

Writing samples and screen shots available

Barbara Danbury

9950 Brockport Road • Houston, Texas 77386

(713) 555-1947 • (713) 555-8590 • barbd@xxx.com

Overview

Commercial applications programmer familiar with large operating environments, database management, direct access technologies, and remote processing. Some exposure to CRT drivers, virtual systems, and database handlers.

Skills

COBOL, BASIC, RPG II, Pascal, C, C Plus

Job Responsibilities

• Program Design
• Coding
• Systems Testing and Debugging
• Creation of Program Documentation

Employers

Houston Savings & Loan, Houston, TX
Programmer/ Analyst
June 1995 - Present

Security Insurance, Dallas, TX
Systems Analyst
May 1993 - June 1995

S & J Manufacturing, Dallas, TX
Programmer
April 1990 - May 1993

Education

B.S. Baylor University, 1990

Major: Computer Science
Minor: Accounting

References Available

Howard L. Meyers

1394 Freeland Road
Des Moines, IA 50309-3023
howardmeyers@xxx.com
(515) 555-1143 Home
(515) 555-4421 Office

Objective: Technical Writing

History: **ADT Business Systems**
Technical Writer   1997 - Present

Achievements: Designed electronic help system for end users as part of larger office automation project. Wrote messages and tied them to proper prompts. Created supplemental online manual for same system. Currently participating in Quality Control Committee reviewing software and suggesting revisions.

Framingham Agricultural Group
Technical Communications Specialist   1995 - 1997

Achievements: Created all manuals, standards, and systems documentation for data processing department. Conducted user experience test groups and implemented changes from findings.

Credentials: B.A. University of Iowa, 1995
Major: English
Minor: Computer Science

Member, Society for Technical Communications

References Available

Maria Frederick

902 Hills Street
Stanford, CA 94305
(415) 555-7194

Overview

Senior systems programmer with more than ten years' experience in data processing, including operations and systems programming.

Hardware/Software

OS/MVS, OS2, CICS, MS/DOS, EASYTRIEVE, CTRLALT, DataEase, INFOSWITCH, VSAM, TSO/ISPF, IMS/DLI, IBM with COPICS/COS package.

Experience

Creative Technologies
Stanford, CA
Senior Systems Programmer
2/97 to Present

Develop and test the company's software products and software development tools, including debuggers, books, and toolkits. Respond to user feedback and participate in revisions and upgrades as necessary.

DataPro Corporation
Boulder, CO
Systems Designer
3/92 to 2/97

Responsible for systems design, maintenance, and modification; disk determination; in-house training of data processors; creation of procedures manual and flowcharts.

Best Data Corporation
Denver, CO
Network Operator
8/90 to 3/92

Installed and maintained terminals, modems, and control units.

Education

B.S.   Data Systems Technologies   1990
         Washington State University

References

Available on Request

Kerri Washington

8273 W. Orlando St.
Knoxville, TN 37917
(615) 555-8233
washington1@xxx.com

Professional Objective

Secure a position in a corporation in which initiative, ambition, and ingenuity are utilized to their full potential.

Qualifications

A demonstrated understanding of the terminology, principles, and theories of Computer/Electrical Engineering. Extensive experience using IBM, Unix, Sys 38 Mod 700, FORTRAN, Basic, Pascal, and Assembly languages. Dedicated work ethic that ensures the highest quality in the most efficient manner.

Work Experience

Programmer Analyst, First National Bank of Tennessee
Researched options and made recommendations for PC-related applications. Interfaced with user departments to develop software.

Programmer Analyst, Victor Group
Developed software to expedite corporate mailings and tracking. Responsible for technical support and maintenance of software product implementation using IMS DB/DC, VSAM, and COBOL.

Quality Engineer, Ashland Microcare
Developed test software consisting of 48 tests for radar antenna systems. Revised test system to reduce testing procedure by three test cycles saving the company over $200,000 in otherwise lost production time.

References Available

RAY PIERCE

3102 HOPPER STREET • CAMBRIDGE, MA 02139
(617) 555-3862 • CELL: (617) 555-9943
EMAIL: RAYPIERCE@XXX.COM

- ## OVERVIEW
More than 12 years of experience in R&D, programming, and systems design. Successful supervisor, recruiter, and trainer.

- ## SKILLS
COBOL, PL/1, RPG III, C, C+, BAL, Ada, CAD/CAM, CICS, IMS/DLI, and VSAM

- ## EXPERIENCE
Triton Electronics
Programmer
6/96 - Present

Assigned to Research and Development Division. Develop and monitor projects, select software and vendors. Recruit and train new employees. Corporation has annual budget of 2.1 million. Currently developing a language interface for E-mail.

Patterson Development Corporation
Computer Technician
4/92 - 6/96

Assisted in development of software package for inventory control. Coded programs for retail use. Experienced in both microcomputer and mainframe environments.

Technical Data Corporation
Systems Designer
5/89 - 4/92

Created custom software for clients requiring specialized business applications. Met with end users to define needs. Designed software and assisted with coding and debugging as requested. Designed and implemented revisions and upgrades based on feedback from product support personnel.

- ## EDUCATION
B.S. Computer Science
Rochester Institute of Technology, 1988

MS Computer and Information Science
Dartmouth, 1990

- ## AFFILIATIONS
American Society for Information Science
Data Processing Management Association

References available upon request

BRADY LICARI

System Programmer • 9283 Michigan St. • Kansas City, MO 64141
(816) 555-6687 • Cell: (816) 555-0092 • Bradylicari@xxx.com

HARDWARE/OPERATING SYSTEMS

IBM 4381, 4341, 3090; OS/MVS/XA, OS/VS1, DOS/VSE, VM, IBM PC/AT

SOFTWARE

CICS, VSAM, IMS/DLI, IDMS/DB-CD, CEDF, BMS, ADS, COBOL, BAL, BASIC, JCL,
TSO/ISPF, ROSCOE

PROFESSIONAL EXPERIENCE

Detmar Control Systems, Kansas City, MO
Systems Manager. Supervised department of 12 Senior P/A and Project Leaders.
Responsible for supporting all systems including emergency reaction, regularly scheduled
maintenance, and upgrades. Oversaw sales and payroll capture, performance and appraisal
reporting, variable rate structures, CICS (controls, adjustments, and reporting).

Digital Systems Design, St. Louis, MO
Developed expertise in CICS, IMS/DLI, and VSAM by interfacing new programs and exits
with the IBM COPICS/COS package. Enhanced MACRO level programs under CICS 1.1.
Wrote several VSAM update and reporting programs. Managed 13 programmers.

Campbell's Department Store, St. Louis, MO
Programmed in COBOL, BAL, and ISAM on accounts receivable projects. Replaced card-
oriented system. Analyzed mail order and catalog system and made appropriate system
upgrades to enhance productivity.

REFERENCES

Andrew Johnson
President, Detmar Control Systems
(816) 555-2255
andrewjohnson@xxx.com

Betty Christenson
Managing Partner, Digital Systems Design
(314) 555-0223
bettychristenson@xxx.com

Arthur C. Elliot

622 Lexington Street   (212) 555-2003 Home
New York, NY 100119   (212) 555-4413 Office

Computer Educator

- Seminars and Individual Tutoring
- Educational Publishing Experience
- Knowledge of COBOL and BASIC
- Experience with microcomputers and mainframes
- B.A. from Syracuse University in English & Computer Science

Experience

Editor
Brighton Publishing, 4/97 to Present

Collaborate with programmers to review educational software and develop manuals. Create computer-aided instruction packages. Work closely with graphics, marketing, and sales staff.

Instructor
MDT Computer Consulting Inc., 6/94 to 4/97

Developed and presented training seminars to teach end-users about microcomputer software packages. Experience with one-on-one tutoring and corporate presentations for 200+ employees.

Owner
Ace Computer Camp, 6/92 to 6/94

Operated high-tech camp (during summer and school breaks). Served 60 students per session in both basic and enrichment programs. Developed curriculum. Trained and supervised four instructors. Oversaw all daily operations.

References Available

Martha Smith

309 Afton Road
Camp Hill, AL 36850
(205) 555-8964
marthamydear@xxx.com

Skills/Experience

- Knowledge of BAL, CICS, CFMS, COBOL, DL/1
- Troubleshooting and repair of PCs, mainframes, and peripheral devices
- Installation, calibration, and testing of electronic field hardware for telecommunications systems
- Training of programmers and maintenance personnel
- Software development for various business applications, including manufacturing, inventory control, scheduling, and cost accounting systems

Employers

Computer Masters Inc.   Whitman Telecommunications
Instructor -- 2 years   Programmer -- 2 years
                               Systems Designer -- 3 years

Data Solutions
Software Designer -- 4 years,

Education

B.S. Computer Science
University of Georgia

Certificate of Completion
Computer Maintenance & Repair Program
Syntex Technical Institute

REFERENCES AVAILABLE

JEAN A. JENKINS

216 S. Fulton Street • Park Ridge, IL 60068
708-555-2461 • Cell: 708-555-5463 • jeanjenkins@xxx.com

PROFESSIONAL BACKGROUND

DB2 Database Administrator/Programmer/Analyst

TECHNICAL EXPERTISE

Databases:	DB2
Languages:	COBOL, Easytrieve Plus, SAS, C, PASCAL, Lisp, Assembler
Systems:	MVS/ESA, MVS/OS, OS/2, IBM/370 (VM/CMS), VAX/VMS, UNIX, PC (Windows, DOS)
Hardware:	IBM mainframe and PCs
PC Software:	System Architect, Word Perfect, Lotus 1-2-3, Dbase IV, Microsoft Office
Other Tools:	Omegamon for DB2, ICandle DB2 tools, OS JCL, TSO/SPF, CICS, VSAM, FileAid, Panvalet, SYSD, SYSM

EDUCATION

B.S. from Northeastern Illinois University
Major: Information science   Minor: Business

Total GPA: 4.9/5.0   GPA in Major: 5.0/5.0

WORK HISTORY

MUNROE INSURANCE, Lincolnwood, IL   4/91 to Present
Senior Database Administrator   2/94 to Present

Support DB2 testing and production activities. Build and maintain Enterprise Data Model for all group systems DB2 applications, using System Architect. Monitor and tune DB2 system and applications to prevent resource shortages and shorten the execution times of long-running queries. Manage DB2 datasets to ensure proper sizing, back-up, organization, and record keeping, preventing problems with space, recovery, and performance. Perform recovery and security functions as required; some involvement with master disaster recovery plan. Maintain common procs (compiles), sample programs, and subroutines (error routines, date functions).

MUNROE INSURANCE (continued)
ACHIEVEMENTS
- Revised DB2 programming standards as member of DB2 development committee.
- Wrote and maintained in-house System Architect programmer training manual and shop data modeling standards.
- Most recently involved in year-long joint effort between Systems and Actuarial to build a DB2-based financial system. Focused on data design, writing SAS macros, and implementing special scheduling system.

Programmer/Analyst   4/91 to 1/94

Supported various group insurance applications.

ACHIEVEMENTS
- Designed and implemented covered person dependents function for administration system, using batch COBOL and CICS applications.
- Converted premium and claim statistical system from sequential files to DB2, for end-user query.
- Rewrote VSAM-based batch COBOL interface to copy covered persons data from administration system to Claimfacts system files.

REFERENCES AVAILABLE

Patrick C. Carter

1617 Emory Street

Forsyth, GA 31029

Patcarter@xxx.com

Professional Goal

Procure a Computer Programmer/Analyst Position

Education

B.S. Quantitative and Information Science
University of Georgia, 1995

Technical Skills

Languages: COBOL, Easytrieve Plus, BASIC, Pascal, C, C+
Databases: DB2, IDMS, RAMIS, Oracle (PC)
Systems: MVS/OS, MS-DOS
Hardware: IBM 4381, 4341, 370/158, Amdahl, PC Compatibles
Tools: TSO/ISPF, CICS, TELON, FILEAID, PANVALET, LIBRARIAN,
             ROSCOE, UCC7, INFOPAC

Work History

RTP Chemical, Forsyth, GA
September 1995 to Present
Programmer Analyst

Responsible for financial systems, including D&B Fixed Assets and D&B Millennium systems and RTP-generated accounts payable, general ledger, check reconciliation, and cash management systems.

Achievements
- Installed latest version of D&B Fixed Assets and D&B Millennium Multi-Mill with query print
- Implemented D&B FA on-line
- Converted RTP's joint venture partner's assets from Global's Fixed Asset system to D&B FA

Taylor Business Group, Atlanta, GA
May 1993 to September 1995
Consultant

Installed, tested, and maintained Millennium accounts payable, general
ledger, and fixed assets. Projects included the conversion of Millennium 1.0
applications to Millennium 2.0 counterparts (MILL, AP, GL, FA), year-end AP
1099 tape installation and support, GL year-end support, and installation
of various bug-fix tapes and hand fixes. Involved in all aspects of project
lifecycles, including writing program specifications for other members
to complete.

Lee & Jacobsen Manufacturing, Atlanta, GA
March 1990 to May 1993
Programmer/Analyst

Responsible for financial systems. Installed and maintained various releases
of Millennium accounts payable, general ledger, purchase order, and fixed
assets. Involved in designing and writing interfaces from other in-house
systems into these M&D systems. Wrote several programs that automated
maintenance procedures and simplified system interfaces.

Springfield Transport, Springfield, IL
March 1988 to March 1990
Programmer/Analyst

Responsible for maintenance and development of mainframe systems and all
PC systems. Wrote mainframe systems in COBOL and command level CICS.
PC software was written in BASIC for use by customers and sales staff.

References on Request

ANDREW MAHONEY

4815 S. Crest Avenue
Ann Arbor, Ml 48766
(313) 555-9874

Goal: Professional Computer Analyst Position

Technical Expertise

Languages:	COBOL, Easytrieve Plus, BASIC, Pascal, C
Databases:	DB2, IDMS, RAMIS, Oracle (PC)
Systems:	IBM, MS/OS, MS-DOS
Tools:	TSO/ISPF, CICS, TELON, FileAid, PANVALET, LIBRARIAN, ROSCOE, CA7, INFOPAC
Packages:	D&B Millennium, AP, GL, FA, ASIPO

Education

B.S. Quantitative and Information Science
University of Michigan, January, 1993

Programmer/Analyst Positions

American Chemical Inc., Ann Arbor, 9/99 to Present

Duties:
- Install and program financial systems
- Test, code, and debug programs
- Create program specifications for project teams

Wright & Stevens Consulting Inc., Ann Arbor, 5/97 to 9/99

Duties:
- Converted financial programming systems
- Handled data conversion projects DB2, TELON, and Easytrieve Plus

Kessler Software, Chicago, 3/95 to 5/97

Duties:
- Installed and maintained financial systems
- Designed and wrote interfaces

TDK International, Chicago, 3/93 to 3/95

Duties:
- Maintained and developed mainframe and PC systems using COBOL, CICS, and BASIC

References Available

Mike McGear

28875 126th Place
Kent, WA 98031
(360) 555-1122
mikemac@xxx.com

Objective

To apply my experience in the electronics field to improve the profitability and efficiency of an established organization.

Professional Background

1996 - Present
Operations Supervisor
Act as liaison between Operations and Programming departments. Ensure verification of system status checks and modems and perform IML on central processing unit. Generate daily reports on status of systems.

1994 - 1996
Computer Maintenance
Monitored PC banks with 20 IBM and 3M printers. Implemented system-wide memory upgrade. Selected and installed new software and acted as troubleshooter.

1993 - 1994
Computer Operator/Data Entry
Updated all ledgers for customer service department, including accounting, payroll, and production.

References

Jeff Atkinson
Supervisor, Dataplus Systems
(360) 555-3323
jeffatkinson@xxx.com

Sheri Ahmed
VP of Operations, QuickStar, Inc.
(360) 555-7773
sheria@xxx.com

Drew Washington
Manager, Instant Action Supplies
(360) 555-1232
drewwashington@xxx.com

George Kusaka

4470 Grant Street • San Francisco, CA 94107
(415) 555-8635 Home • (415) 555-4800 Office • gkusaka@xxx.com

Objective: A senior programmer/analyst position developing and maintaining computer applications, with opportunity to develop skills in PC-based applications

Skills: MVS JES 3, Expediter, FileAid, Endeavor, COBOL II, DB2, IBM 3033 DOS/VSE, EMC2 Disk, CICS 1.7/VSAM, CS-Sort, CA-DART, System Manager, FALCON, COBOL, IBM 3083 MVS-XA TSO/ISPF, COBOL, IMS-DB, VSAM, PANVALET, JCL, Utilities, EASYTRIEVE, ABEND-AID, MS DOS 6.22, Windows, Office 97 & 2000, WordPerfect, ABC Flowchart, SuperProject Plus, Lotus 1-2-3 & Notes

Experience: BIGELOW BROTHERS 8/98 to Present

Developed and revised online management tool used to calculate bonus pay for sales associates. Created other customer service reports. Nonproduction applications under INFORMIX 46L.

SOFTWARE MONTHLY 8/96 to 8/98

Developed Ad Ticket application and order conversion for the ADMARC computer package, used to centrally administer 150,000 magazine advertisements annually, plus receivables. System replaced four separate legacy systems.

PASCAL PRINTERS   2/93 to 8/96

Handled maintenance and enhancement of labor/cost system for ten plants. Developed online job-class-exception subsystem and the online file maintenance for the same system. Developed credit approval system for Accounts Receivable to help track customer credit profiles and customers' parent corporations. The customer credit approval report became the internal executive level document for credit administration.

Education: B.S. Information Science
                     Kenyon College
                     January, 1993

References: Submitted upon request

Lucas Jackson
2399 S. Division • Grand Rapids, MI 49503
(616) 555-9354
Cell: (616) 555-2819
lucasjackson@xxx.com

Objective

Apply my skills as a content expert to a new challenge with a company focused on quality, dedication, and ingenuity.

Work

1998 to present

Content Strategist, Sonic Consulting, Grand Rapids, MI

Provide digital solutions for clients interested in establishing their presence online. Make recommendations on content assets, third-party content partnerships, and content management systems. Direct copywriters and design teams to fulfill the clients' objectives and create brand strategies.

1996 to 1998

Website Manager, *Crash! Magazine*, Detroit, MI

Directed the online version of *Crash! Magazine* and ensured that design and content guidelines of the site followed those of the print version. Coordinated special events to drive traffic to the site resulting in a 75 percent increase in hits over four months. Created and edited content specifically for the site to establish its own identity.

1994 to 1996

Writer, *Digital City Magazine*, Detroit, MI

Researched and wrote articles covering the emerging Internet business and issues that relate to that unique business sector. Interviewed people involved in cutting-edge development on the Web and analyzed the business implications of this unique medium.

Skills

- Intimate familiarity with standard style guides including *AP*, *Chicago Manual*, *MLA*, and *Wired*.
- Very knowledgeable in the use and merits of content management systems such as Vignette, ePrise, and BroadVision.
- Uncanny ability to merge creative vision with business objectives to create distinctive and engaging content.

References available upon request

Elaine Smith

1511 West Street • Boston, MA 02116

(617) 555-4192

elainesmith@xxx.com

Goal

Programmer/analyst position with opportunity to develop skills in software design.

Skills

CICS, OS2, COBOL II, FileAid, OS/MVS, MS/DOS, EASYTRIEVE, Data Ease, INFOSWITCH, VSAM, TSO/ISPF, DOS/VSE, DOS JCL, Dylacor, OS/VMS FALCON

Work History

Colonial Insurance
Programmer, 8/96 to Present

Developed mainframe programs to create a download file for a PC-based pension administration package. Converted and maintained the raw material paper inventory system that tracked $9 million paper inventory, from a Honeywell DPS-88 platform to an IBM.

Williams Financial Group
Programmer, 6/93 to 8/96

Programmer and project manager for wholesale finance core system. Developed front-end processor to reformat invoice information into trust finance agreements using multiple IMS databases. While project manager, also directed activities of general ledger group.

Education

Boston College, Bachelor of Science Degree, awarded June 1993
Major: Finance
Minor: Computer and Information Science

References

Personal and professional references available

AMY DENNING

763 Richardson Road
Menlo Park, California 94025
(415) 555-3273
Cell: (415) 555-3527

EMPLOYMENT HISTORY

7/98 to Present
Owner/Denning Translation Services

Own and manage document translation service offering document translation into all languages. Provide WP and DTP services to clients in medical, legal, and business community worldwide. Employ staff of five data processors and one programmer. Oversee accounts payable and receivable.

6/95 to 7/98
Systems Analyst/Ryerson Technical Support

Database management consultant and data programmer. Created database files and flowcharts for business applications. Produced monthly systems status reports and weekly programming goals. Reconfigured software for systems compatibility, compiled programs in BASIC, C, Pascal, and FOR-TRAN. Worked with Hardware Design Team on large systems conversion projects.

TECHNICAL SKILLS

COBOL, COBOL II, BASIC, C, Pascal, FORTRAN, Lotus 1-2-3 and Notes, PL/1, LISP, ALGOL, GPSS

CREDENTIALS

B.S. University of Denver, Computer Science, 1995
Member, Association of Computer Programmers and Analysts

References Available

CORBIN DREYFUS
7530 Cypress Street • Midlothian, VA 23113 • (804) 555-7154 • corbind@xxx.com

Overview

- Successful computer consultant
- Knowledge of BASIC, C Language, MS/DOS, COBOL, FORTRAN, Pascal, DOS/VSE, IBM 370 under OS/MVS and JES3
- Specialize in long-term corporate consulting/training projects
- B.S., University of Virginia, Information Sciences, 1995

Recent Projects

QDC INTERNATIONAL
6/98 to Present

Provide freelance technical support. Job has included systems analysis to determine needs, selection of microcomputers and peripheral equipment, installation of hardware, design of custom software. Train employees in use of commercial packages, including file-handling program.

MIDLOTHIAN COMMERCIAL BANK
4/97 to 6/98

Hired to devise and implement quality control procedures. Designed, staffed, and implemented program. Trained and evaluated in-house staff in use of new procedures.

SAWYER BUSINESS SYSTEMS
3/95 to 4/97

Successfully designed and implemented schema and subsystem flow for inventory subsystem. Created and documented microcomputer hardware and software standards, saving the company more than $50,000 in first year of implementation.

VIRGINIA PUBLIC SCHOOLS,
Districts 62 and 14
3/93 to 3/95

Designed computer labs for four public high schools and six elementary schools. Project included developing and presenting proposal, selecting equipment, soliciting bids, supervising installation of hardware, and training teaching staff.

References Available

Annie Peters
Procedures Analyst

26665 Allison Rd.
Peyton, CO
80831

(719) 555-2211
(719) 555-8200
anniepeters@xxx.com

Professional Experience

IntraCom, Peyton, CO
Procedures Analyst
Coordinated teams for trouble shooting and problem tracking. Monitored and supervised those teams. Created quality assurance program to reduce product deficiencies. Interfaced with Senior Level Management from various departments to address their needs and unique product failures and to establish custom solutions.

Associate Systems Analyst
Oversaw vital aspects of quality control operations. Contributed to overall success of the department and ensured proper staffing. Coordinated the activities of the manufacturing personnel for two departments (three shifts). Supervised 20 quality control employees, monitored their reports, and implemented corrective actions. Updated and drafted new procedures to improve systemwide efficiency.

Haliburt Manufacturing, Peyton, CO
Senior Quality Control Technician
Supervised 8 Quality Control technicians, overseeing draft schedules and performance evaluations, and troubleshooting problems. Coordinated audits for departments, trained new technicians, and conducted tests for certification.

Education

University of Colorado, Boulder, CO
B.S., Engineering, 1993

References Available

DANIEL THRELKELD

4412 Trask Road
Hasbrouck Heights, NJ 07606
(201) 555-2102
threkeld101@xxx.com

TECHNICAL SKILLS

UNIX, C, Pascal, FORTRAN, BASIC, AutoCAD, COBOL, LISP, DOS/VSE, TSO, VSAM

EDUCATION

M.I.S. Degree, University of California, Berkeley
B.S. in Mathematics, University of California, Berkeley

EXPERIENCE

Grove Software
4/97 to Present
Software Engineer

Duties: Develop software specifications, create custom software, handle extensive customer interface and user training, provide product descriptions and training to in-house marketing and sales staff.

Global Manufacturing
2/95 to 4/97
Project Manager

Duties: Participated in product support and development as member of microcomputer design team. Created product specifications, designed upgrades for existing product, supported marketing efforts for software and hardware product lines.

Kerby Business Systems
1/92 to 2/95
Systems Engineer

Duties: Programmed manufacturing systems, including enhancement of real-time systems and support of current and updated systems throughout conversion phase.

References Available

Jill Eisenberg

261 Merrill Street • Cleveland, Ohio 44138
(216) 555-4034 • jilly@xxx.com

Summary

Experienced technical services supervisor with experience in UNISYS equipment, NCP/VTAM and CICS systems programming, mainframe/transactions database environments.

Technical Skills

DOS/VSE, CICS, DL1, IMS, VTAM, NCP, EASYTRIEVE, ASSEMBLER, COBOL, MS/DOS, BASIC, VSAM, IDMS/B-DC, CEDF, BMS, INTERTEST, EZTEST, ADS

Employers

Trask Technical Services   4/97 to Present
Reynolds Software   5/95 to 4/97
Stevens Pharmaceuticals   4/94 to 5/95

Achievements

- Designed and created new Data Support Center in branch office. Installed and tested all new mainframes, PCs, peripherals. Coordinated data transfer from home office.
- Supervised 10-member Data Processing Department using UNISYS equipment for data entry and output.
- Maintained 200-terminal communications network.
- Provided technical support for large online batch order-processing system.

References Available

Michelle Tyler

3116 Ventura Street
Morton, PA 19070
(610) 555-4611
mtyler@xxx.com
Programmer/Analyst

Experience

6/98 to Present
Senior Systems Analyst
Corporate Software Inc.

Design software for business applications including invoice and order processing. Also create tape processing for credit bureaus and federal agencies. Most programming done in COBOL using DEC VAX 11/780 hardware.

5/96 to 6/98
MIS Specialist
R & J Manufacturing

Directed MIS group providing computer services for all in-house business applications. Designed and implemented online inventory and distribution system responsible for $45,000 annual savings.

6/94 to 5/96
Customer Service Technician
Ultimate Software Inc.

Provided product support for end users of Ultimate Software products including spreadsheets, word processing programs, database programs, and graphics applications. Pinpointed and solved callers' problems. Alerted technical writers to need for revisions.

Education

B.S. Information Science   Pennsylvania State University 1987

Knowledge of IBM, Compaq, and Apple PCs; COBOL, DEC VAX 11/780, BASIC, C, FORTRAN, NATURAL, Pascal, CICS, DOS/VSE, DOS/JCL, TSO, and VSAM

References

Available on Request

Katrina Parker

1402 Greenbriar Road

Charleston, WV 25304

(304) 555-1704

Applications & Systems Programmer

Credentials

- B.S. in Computer Science—March 1995—University of Michigan; minor in Accounting
- Knowledge of COBOL, FORTRAN, Pascal, C, C Plus, BASIC, PRG II, CAD/CAM, RPG II, ASSEMBLY language #68000, 8086 & 6502, and dbase
- High level of self-motivation and attention to detail

Job Duties

- Code, test, debug, and maintain programs
- Create program documentation
- Integrate new hardware into existing systems
- Diagnose and correct systems failures
- Maintain monitors, database packages, compilers, assemblers, utility programs
- Select and modify new hardware and software to company specifications

---

Achievements

- Designed programs in C Plus for Heritage Bank to coordinate functions of ATM machines
- Purchased new hardware and software for Advantage Publishers; modified equipment to suit company's needs and resolve interoperability issues

---

Employers

Heritage Bank	6/99 to Present
Advantage Publishers	4/96 to 6/99

References

Marta Dalton	Renu Das
Vice President of Finance	Director of Human Resources
Heritage Bank	Advantage Publishers
411 Watkins Street	694 Dale Street
Charleston, WV 25304	Deer Park, NY 11729
(304) 555-2225, ext. 203	(516) 555-7937

Steven Stone

390 Fawn Road
Tequesta, Florida 33469
(407) 555-5754
stevestone@xxx.com

Background

Software engineer with extensive experience in C/UNIX programming for variety of business applications. Multi-language experience in both PCs and mainframes. Design through implementation.

Software

COBOL	APS	BAL
FileAid	FORTRAN	M BASIC
PL1	RPG II	CICS MACRO
DBASE II	DL/1	DMS
CPM	GCOS	DOS/JCL
OS/MVS	OS/MVS/XA	MS/DOS
JES 3	BDAM	ISAM
ROSCOE	TSO	EXEC
XEDIT	ETHERNET	BASIC

Employers

Herald Computer Design	6/98 to Present
Southwest Software	7/95 to 6/98
MicroTel Express	4/94 to 7/95
Brighton Telecommunications	5/91 to 4/94

Achievements

- Designed user interface for PC file manager
- Used Vista program to create windowing environment for IBM PC under MS/DOS
- Led Quality Control Team responsible for successfully upgrading invoicing system using DB/2 and COBOL
- Developed software for several manufacturing, inventory, distribution, and cost-accounting systems using CFMS data structures in both BAL and COBOL
- Received Quality Control Award from MicroTel Express

Education

B.S. Computer Science
University of Washington, Tacoma

REFERENCES AVAILABLE

Samantha Goldblum

7668 N. Milwaukee Ave.
Chicago, IL 60623
(773) 555-4678
samanthagoldblum@xxx.com

"One of the most thorough and innovative Information Architects we've had on staff. A real asset to any company"

--Tim Andrews,
Director of Information Technology, Mayweather Consulting.

Education

Bachelors of Arts, English with a minor in Mass Communications
University of Chicago, 1996

Professional Development

March 1998 to Present
Information Architect, Mayweather Consulting, Chicago
Develop compelling website architecture with an emphasis on user experience. Employ tested and accepted user experience methodology to ensure the sites are up to standard Web practice. Arrange data on sites in a logical manner to ensure the user finds the information he is looking for.

May 1996 to March 1998
Web Master, *Modern Chicago Living* magazine, Chicago
Created online experience to promote print version of *Modern Chicago Living* magazine. Mapped out the entire site and built it from the ground up with tech staff. Edited and adjusted content to fit the digital experience. Developed online marketing strategy to drive traffic to the site.

References

Tim Andrews
Director of Information Technology, Mayweather Consulting.
(312) 555-2932
timandrews@xxx.com

Nancy Mayweather
CEO, Mayweather Consulting
(312) 555-9923
nancymayweather@xxx.com

John Bennett
Editor, *Modern Chicago Living* magazine
(773) 555-1112
johnbennett@xxx.com

KAREN MARTIN

899 Exler Street
Jenkinstown, PA 19046
(215) 555-8870 Home
(215) 555-0816 Office

TECHNICAL SKILLS

FORTRAN	BASIC	PL 1
COBOL	RPG II	CICS MACRO
Pascal	APS	D BASE II
C	BAL	DL/1
C Plus	FileAID	DMS
VSAM	LISP	ALGOL

RECENT ACHIEVEMENTS

- Created printer input/output service routines in FORTRAN for IBM-compatible retail terminal
- Designed software interface in C Plus for new multifunction printer
- Converted Accounts Payable's TCAM data system to centralized, online CICS system

SYSTEMS PROGRAMMER/ANALYST POSITIONS

Regional Telephone Company
Jenkinstown, PA
June 1998 to Present

Lexington Insurance Company
Pittsburgh, PA
May 1995 to June 1998

Williams Manufacturing
Pittsburgh, PA
April 1992 to May 1995

EDUCATION

B.S. Information Science
University of Virginia
GPA 4.8/5.0

REFERENCES

Personal and professional references on request

Robert Capa

42 Park Avenue • New York, NY USA • (212) 555-7783 • robertcapa@xxx.com

Web Designer

I design eye catching, innovative websites that engage the user, promote the client's brand, and create a buzz. I seamlessly integrate functionality into form.

History

Sloan Digital, New York City

In my three years at Sloan, I have designed award winning websites for 8 Fortune 100 companies and 14 other industry leaders. Two sites I designed were featured in *Fast Business* and *Wired* magazines. My attention to detail and eye for design has made me the lead designer on my companyís biggest projects.

Sunday Media Solutions, Denver

Over the course of four years, I proved myself as an innovative designer with a watchful eye on deadlines and was promoted from Junior Designer to Lead Designer. My expertise in e-commerce made me an invaluable asset to Sunday Media. My desire to live in New York led me from my native Denver to bigger clients and more responsibility.

Carter Consulting Group, Denver

Carter is where my career began as an intern at one of Denver's most respected and established consulting firms. Under the tutelage of Don Balmore I honed my skills as a designer and established myself as a key staff member.

Education

Swift School of Visual Arts, Denver, CO
New York University, Masters of Visual Arts

References and samples available

JOHN HERNANDEZ

916 Baker Street
East Greenwich, RI 02818
(401) 555-6208
jhernandez@xxx.com

Objective

Software Engineering

Technical Skills

C, Unix systems, VMS, MS/DOS, Pascal, BASIC, Macro II, IBM 370, Cyber 175, VAX-11/780, IBM VM/CMS

Employers

Cross Computer Equipment, 9/97 - Present

Creative Software Inc., 8/94 - 9/97

Newton Educational Group, 7/91 - 8/94

Achievements

- Created I/0 interface between Intel 8086 software and 8031 hardware
- Developed and maintained file transfer using C on DEC VAX 11/780
- Created primary interface for marketing and sales staffs for support of software products line
- Served as project leader for custom software development
- Promoted from programmer to senior programmer within one year

Education

B.S. Computer Science, University of Maine, 1991

References Available

Daniel S. Hall

974 Voyager Court
Clayton, MO 63105
Danhall@xxx.com
(314) 555-4730

Overview

Experienced computer consultant with background in:

- MIS development
- EDP audits and conversion projects
- Installation of mainframe and micro systems
- Technical writing

Employers

KNC DATA
Senior Technical Writer, 1998 to Present

Develop operations manuals, simplifying technical systems specifications for end users. Acquire necessary data and specifications from engineers, programmers, and systems analysts. Edit and revise as necessary for final corporate approval prior to publication.

HUDSON CONSULTANTS
MIS specialist, 1996 to 1998

Assisted with all aspects of information management for new firm. Selected systems vendor and supervised installation of equipment. Established financial, organizational, and documentation procedures. Hired and trained personnel.

REMINGTON BUSINESS SYSTEMS
Consultant, 1994 to 1996

Coordinated transition to new site and established upgraded Data Processing Department. Responsibilities included equipment installation, creation of documentation standards, data I/0 control, and production scheduling.

Credentials

M.B.A. Rutgers University
B.S. New York University

Knowledge of COBOL, Pascal, FORTRAN, RPG II, Unisys systems, EASYTRIEVE, FileAid, C, C Plus, Lotus Notes, WordPerfect, MSDOS, Unix

REFERENCES AVAILABLE

Monique Trudeau

322 N. Shore Dr. • Miami Beach, FL 33140
(305) 555-3225 • Cell: (305) 555-7298
Moniquetrudeau@xxx.com

Objective: Secure employment as a computer programmer in the software field with opportunities for professional growth and advancement

Education: Michigan Institute of Technology, Houghton, MI
B.A. Computer Science, May 1995

Technical Experience: IBM 370, VM/CMS, XEDIT, DEC-10, IBM PC, DOS, DBASE I, PASCAL, ASSEMBLER, FORTRAN, COBOL, LISP, SNOBOL, BASIC, WORD, Lotus Notes.

Professional Experience: 01/96 to Present
Technical Programmer, Reynolds Electronics, Bradenton, FL
Responsible for designing, writing, and implementation of software systems using appropriate databases. Integrate database packages and operating systems. Train and manage new personnel. Recommend hardware and software upgrades.

10/94 to 01/96
Technical Programmer, Springfield Manufacturing, Miami Beach, FL
Designed and wrote new applications and made enhancements to existing programs. Unit and system testing, debugging, and implementation as well as writing documentation.

Programming Consultant, Michigan Institute of Technology Computer Lab
Helped students and faculty design, modify, and debug their programs. Provided technical advice and recommended software.

References: Gary Halman
Vice President, Production, Reynolds Electronics
(813) 555-3344
garyhalman@xxx.com

Phyllis Lin
CEO, Springfield Manufacturing
(305) 555-3209
phyllislin@xxx.com

Prof. Michael Lee
Head of Computing Services, Michigan Institute of Technology
(906) 555-8883
mikelee@xxx.com

Other references available upon request.

Neal Redman

618 N. Trinity Lane   (617) 555-6824 Home
Boston, MA 02129   (617) 555-2400 Work

Goal

Systems Programmer/Analyst Position

Skills

IBM/DB&DC	CICS
DB2	COBOL
ROSCOE	IFPS
EASYTRIEVE	EASYTRIEVE Plus
VSAM	IMS/DLI
BAL	BASIC
JCL	ROSCOE

Summary

- Ten years' systems programming/analysis experience using IBM workstations
- Proven record of meeting deadlines
- Supervised for 8-member data processing department
- Programmed applications in support of Inventory Management System
- Converted interface to Accounts Receivable System from MSA to M&D, including development of necessary program specifications
- Designed, implemented, and supported various subsystems using CICS, COBOL, and EASYTRIEVE Plus
- Managed user queries as customer service technician

Employers

Waverly Insurance   1996 - Present
Stanford Business Group   1994 - 1996

Education

Master's in Information Science
Massachusetts Institute of Technology

Bachelor's in Accounting; minor in Computer Science
Boston College

References

Business and personal references available

allison moore
Computer Repair Technician

6556 Crosstown Pkwy.
Cherry Hill, NJ 08003
(609) 555-6189
allisonmoore@xxx.com

goal

To apply my new education in computer repair to a new challenge in a company focused on quality.

education

Stevenson Technical School, Newark, NJ
Received certificate 9/2000. Curriculum included: Mathematics, Basic Electricity, AC & DC Circuitry, Power Supplies, Semiconductor Theory and Troubleshooting, Operational Amplifiers, Boolean Algebra, Combination Logic Circuits, Flip Flops, Memory Systems, D/A Conversion, and Microprocessors.

professional experience

DoubleTech, Inc., Newark, NJ
11/96 to Present
Field Service trained on high-speed check processing unit, which included optical reader, magnetic ink character reader, and ink jet printer. Also worked on 80 megabyte Pertec disk drives, line printers, and Harris PC6 controllers.

Schector Electronics, Princeton, NJ
04/95 to 11/96
Worked from blueprints, pictorials, and schematics reading and interpreting changes made by engineers in regard to the modification of circuits. Worked well alone and in groups to ensure all changes were made. Awarded two certificates of achievement for lowest failure rate two quarters in a row.

References Available

KEITH LAWRENCE

450 Stewart Street • Louisville, CO 80027
Keithlawrence@xxx.com
(303) 555-0635 Home • (303) 555-4506 Office

Professional Process and Systems Engineering

Overview

Seasoned professional seeking computer engineering position. Extensive work with COBOL, Pascal, and BASIC. Background in software development, systems support, revision of batch systems, and implementation of automatic assembly systems.

Employers

Morton Technical Services
Systems Engineer, **1998 to Present**

Duties: Support existing and upgraded systems throughout conversion projects. Use of EDP and MIS technologies extensively. Revise and upgrade batch systems. Diagnose and correct error messages. Handle customer service duties. Train in-house users.

Computech Computer Equipment Inc.
Systems Programmer, **1995 to 1998**

Duties: Systems programming. Converted software products to Computech operating systems with assistance of applications programmers. Developed advanced systems/applications interfaces.

Education

B.S.   Computer Science
California State University 1995
GPA: 4.8/5.0

References

Gary Simms
President
Morton Technical Systems
303-555-4894
gsimms@xxx.com

Elizabeth Stark
Senior Systems Engineer
Computech
303-555-0595, ext. 311
elizabeth@xx.com

Andrew Kohltar

19 Desierto Rd. • El Paso, NM 79912
(915) 555-2290 • andrewkohltar@xxx.com
Computer Graphic Designer

Skills

Adobe: Photoshop, PageMaker, Illustrator
Quark Xpress
Flash
DreamWeaver
Freehand
Micrografx Simply 3D
All Microsoft Applications, including PowerPoint, Excel, and Word
Web Design with HTML, XTML, Javascript

Design Experience

Shock! Interactive, 9/98 to Present
Graphic Design Lead
Create packaging and Web designs for several Fortune 500 clients. Meet with clients
and lead brainstorming sessions to develop visual online presence. Establish design
guidelines for clients to use on future campaigns to ensure brand consistency. Pitch
new business proposal to perspective clients. Produce eye-catching, cutting-edge
design comps under tight deadlines and within proposed budgets.

DDM Electronic Media Design, 4/96 to 9/98
Visual Arts Specialist
Employed cutting-edge Web design tools to design and create logos, banner ads,
and interactive games to increase site traffic to clients' sites. Married companies'
business goals to their creative direction to create online buzz and increase
"stickiness" of websites.

Cooper, White and Dennison Design, 6/94 to 4/96
Graphic Designer
Developed logos, labels, and Point of Purchase (POP) designs for local leading
businesses. Designed pitch materials including slides, PowerPoint Presentations,
and signage resulting in new business wins totaling more than $4 million.

Waterhouse Design Firm, 11/91 to 6/94
Assistant Designer
Helped create layouts and storyboards for sales presentations. Proofed and corrected
fliers, postcards, and webcards for large-scale ad campaigns.

References available
Design samples available

Belinda White

6204 Oceanview Drive
Ormond Beach, FL 32176
(904) 555-8211
bwhite@xxx.com

Summary

Data processing expertise with specialization in DB2 and CICS analysis, design, and development.

Technical Background

Languages:	COBOL, Pascal, BAL, BASIC, FORTRAN, SQL
Systems:	MVS/ESA, MVS/JCL, DOS/VS/VSE, MS/DOS
Software:	VSAM, CICS, DB2, IMS DB, TSO/SPF/ISPF, UNIX, WYLBUR, JCL, DOS
Hardware:	IBM PCs and compatibles

Employment Record

Consultant   **K&R Distributors**
7/96 to Present   **Ormond Beach, Florida**

Design, test, and execute COBOL statements for heavy report requests, ensuring proper syntax and logic. Create and modify specifications. Logical and physical design. Structural procedures testing.

Systems Analyst   **Barrington Financial Group**
6/94 to 7/96   **Miami, Florida**

Upgraded and expanded general ledger system of more than 125 online and batch programs. Established operational procedures and created systems documentation.

Systems Programmer   **Warner Industries**
8/91 to 6/94   **Key West, Florida**

Developed new Order Entry application, merging new DB2 tables and views with existing database.

Education

B.S. Computer Science
Syracuse University   1991

Courses
• Advanced Systems Programming and Analysis
• COBOL, BAL, FORTRAN, and BASIC Programming
• CICS Fundamentals and Applications Programming
• Technical Writing

References Available

Mohammed Sharif

1779 N. Madison St.
Washington, D.C. 20036
(202) 555-4445
mohammedsharif@xxx.com

Technical Background

Languages	Systems	Software
COBOL	MVS/JCL	VSAM
COBOL II	MVS/ESA	IBM DB
FORTRAN	EASYTRIEVE	CICS
SQL	DOS/VS/VSE	DB2
BAL	MS DOS	QUICKEN
BASIC		EASE

Professional Summary

More than 5 years of computer programming in professional settings.

Work History

Programmer, Webster Data Inc.

Responsible for the consolidation of information into a database. Create programs to meet requirements of human resources department covering the needs of 10,000 employees. Wrote programs for new HMO system transferring accounts to new system without interruption of coverage and with little disruption to staff.

Applications Programmer, Ctech Inc.

Responsible for designing, coding, and debugging applications for inventory control, sales summary analysis, and stock trafficking. Applications were designed using BLIS/COBOL Version 4.

Education

Columbia University
Computer Science Degree, 1995

References Available

JERRY RESTON
8204 W. Bishop Street • Atlanta, Georgia 30356
(770) 555-7089 Office • (770) 555-6947 Home
jerryreston@xxx.com

OBJECTIVE: **SUMMARY:**	Systems Analysis/Programming Projects • Independent contractor for past 10 years • Specifications writing • Programming for batch processing • Design and coding of new programs • Structural procedure testing • Data and program modifications • Systems testing and debugging • Implementation of business and scientific applications
CLIENTS:	Culver Technical Institute Tredmont Industries Georgia Telecommunications ATP Business Systems Adler Financial Group

TECHNICAL
EXPERTISE:
	Languages: COBOL, COBOL II, FORTRAN,
	                    BAL, Pascal, BASIC
	Systems: MVS/JCL, MVS/ESA, EASYTRIEVE,
	                    DOS/VS/VSE, MS/DOS
	Software: VSAM, IBM, DB, DB2, CICS

EDUCATION:	M.I.S. University of Georgia 1992 B.S. North Park College 1990
REFERENCES:	Bob Carrington Vice President/General Manager ATP Business Systems Telephone: (707) 555-2984 Carol Sawyer Human Resources Director Adler Financial Group Telephone: (707) 555-2280

Benjamin Yoav

1558 Hilsdale Dr.
Los Angeles, CA 90068
(213) 555-2318
Cell: (213) 555-8893
benyoav@xxx.com

Data Analyst

Superior organizational and analytical skills. More than ten years business experience in a variety of settings. A consistent record of systems analysis and programming applications that are easily maintained and consistent in outstanding performance.

Employment

Herron Systems, Los Angeles, CA, April 1998 to Present
Responsible for support of all integrated systems, including subsystems. Developed software configuration management procedures for a variety of systems. Utilize Application Development Workbench to maintain logical and physical data models, data flow diagrams, and structure charts for PC-based system.

Lockhart, Inc., Santa Barbara, CA, June 1996 to April 1998
Developed project standards and procedures as well as trained other employees on system. Conducted modeling sessions with development and user teams for delivery to executive management.

Denali Systems, Inc., Fullerton, CA, October 1993 to June 1996
Coordinated program and CLIST maintenance, testing and implementation for remote users. Trained and supervised junior programmers to maintain and monitor data integrity.

Education

B.S. University of California–Los Angeles, 1993

References Available

Ronald McNeal

2416 Yates Street • Oakbrook, IL 60521
(708) 555-7326 • ronmcneal@xxx.com

SUMMARY

- Fifteen years as technical consultant to finance, healthcare, and manufacturing executives
- Database and online applications programming
- Software design and implementation
- System conversion projects
- Multi-language experience with micros and mainframes

TECHNICAL EXPERIENCE

Hardware
IBM PCs and mainframes, Honeywell, System 38, PC/XT/AT, NCR

Software
COBOL, COBOL II, FileAid, PL/1, CICS, DB2, DOS/VS, VSAM, ROSCOE, ISPF, C, FORTRAN, RPG II, BAL, EASYTRIEVE Plus, Pascal, MS/DOS, BASIC

CLIENTS

Crest Financial Group
Merit Insurance Company
Excel Manufacturing
Security Healthcare

EDUCATION

B.S. Computer Science
Northern Illinois University, 1993

REFERENCES

Personal and professional references submitted on request.

Chris Smith

88743 West Belmont Ave.
Phoenix, AZ 85037
(602) 555-6654
chrissmith@xxx.com

Programmer

Goal

Seeking an entry-level programming position with an established firm.

Education

Arizona State University, Bachelor of Science, May 2001.

Professional Experience

November 1998 to Present
Arizona State University Computer Science Department

> Converted UNISYS environment to an IBM environment for a COBOL/CICS application system. Prepared BMS maps, helped prepare JCL for batch programs as well as several other duties.

Student Supervisor, Arizona State University Computer Lab

> Supervised computer lab help desk staff. Maintained work schedules for 22 student staff members, assisted other students with computer-related problems. Updated software on 50 IBM PCs and 30 Macs.

References available upon request

Hasper Consulting Inc.

Ted Hasper
483 Briar Road
Boulder, CO
(303) 555-6232
tedhasper@xxx.com

Technical Expertise

Hardware	Software	Languages
IBMs	DB2	COBOL
Macintosh	CICS	COBOL II
	SQL	PL/1

Job Skills

- Applications programming—development through implementation
- Database design
- Specifications writing
- Coding in SQL and DB2

Recent Projects

Wexler Chemical Corporation—Data conversion from Unisys to DB2, including design, coding, debugging, and implementation. Interfaces written in CICS and DB2.

Arco Inc.—Team leader for database design project. Created code in DB2 and SQL. Tested and implemented database.

Parker and Reed Accounting—Conversion project shifting general ledger system from IMS to DB2. Programs written in COBOL II with embedded CICS and DB2.

Addington Business Systems—Upgraded applications processing system using programs written in PL/1.

Education

M.I.S. University of Colorado, 1992

B.S. Northern Illinois University, 1989
Accounting major/Computer Science minor

Undergraduate GPA 4.8/5.0
Graduate GPA 5.0/5.0

References Available

Jackie Andrews

8484 Owl Creek Road • Colorado Springs, CO 80919
(719) 555-2397 • jackieandrews@xxx.com

Objective

To find a position as a Local Area Network Manager.

Experience

DataFax, Inc., LAN Specialist, June 1998 to Present
Wrote, tested, and debugged programs. Developed user guide for multiple-user data entry system. Customized user reports and data entry. Trained new users and maintained entire system for outstanding reliability rating.

CCM Systems, Inc., Systems Analyst, November 1995 to June 1998
Created and modified data base files. Technical system used LAN, NCR, DOS, Multiplan, Quattro Pro, and CICS. Provided user training and handled troubleshooting duties.

Technical Skills

Languages: Pascal, Assembler, C, C Plus, Basic, and Prolog
Software: Windows, Microsoft Office, Novell Advanced Netware 286/386 V2.15 Network, DOS, MS-DOS, Excel, Lotus, Adobe Photoshop and PageMaker, Turbo C, Quattro Pro, and dbase III+.

Education

University of Colorado, B.S. Computer Science, 1995

References Available

Leslie Argus

988 Green Street
Des Plaines, IL 60016
(708) 555-9113

Goal

Computer Programming/Systems Analysis

Credentials

Knowledge of COBOL, IMS/DB, SQL, DB2, CICS, BASIC, Unisys Systems, EASYTRIEVE

B.S. in Computer Science from Northwestern University

Work History

Computer Consultant, 1996 to Present

Selected Projects:

- **Amex Software: Six-Month Database Design Project**
  Created customer information database in DB2 for use by Marketing Division.
- **Paddington Insurance Group: One-Year Applications Programming Project**
  Financial applications programming with programs written in COBOL, CICS, and DB2.
- **TNN Manufacturing: Six-Month Conversion Project**
  Shifted financial applications from IMS to DB2 system under tight deadline pressure.
- **Midwest Business Systems: Eight-Month Interface Design Project**
  Designed and installed new general ledger system utilizing PC to mainframe connections.

References

Edith Clark, Amex Software   (708) 555-2600, ext. 262
Martin Blaise, Paddington Insurance   (312) 555-6207
Kevin Alexander, TNN Manufacturing   (708) 555-7302
Dale Serron, Midwest Business Systems   (708) 555-8115

Jack Schultz · 1013 Drexler Street · Stanford, California 94305 · (415) 555-7194

SUMMARY

Senior programmer with extensive experience in both systems and applications programming.

TECHNICAL KNOWLEDGE

COBOL	CICS	MVS/JCL
BASIC	MS/DOS	QUICKEN
Pascal	VSAM	EASYTRIEVE
RPG II	C	C Plus

POSITIONS HELD

Systems Programmer
Hofstra Technical Group
March 1998 to Present

Systems Programmer
Olson Realty Inc.
February 1996 to March 1998

Data Entry Technician
Quality Data Corporation
July 1994 to February 1996

ACHIEVEMENTS

- Suggested key revision to reference manual reducing customer service calls by 10 percent
- Received Hofstra's Employee of the Month Award
- Completed in-house Quality Control Training Program

EDUCATION

Bachelor of Technology (B.T.) Degree
Stanford Technical Institute
June 1994

References Available

Stacey Charles

609 Lincoln Road

Houston, Texas 77386

(713) 555-1947

OBJECTIVE

Computer Programming Position

EDUCATION

Baylor University
B.S. in Computer Science expected June 2002

Coursework in COBOL, BASIC, RPG II, Pascal, C, ISAM, CICS, BMS, as well as other software and languages

GPA of 4.91/5.0

Earned 50 percent of tuition by working while carrying full course load

EMPLOYMENT

1998 - 2001, Computer Lab Assistant, Baylor University

Instructed undergraduates in use of computer hardware and software. Assistance ranged from word-processing instruction to programming assignments.

Summers 1995 - 1998, Sales Associate, Computer World

Sold computer equipment and software. Answered customers' questions. Provided ongoing customer service and training.

REFERENCES AVAILABLE

marcus johnson
733 Sherrill Street
New York, NY 10019
(212) 555-3114
marcusjohnson@xxx.com

summary

Experienced computer educator, with background in educational publishing, offering corporate training programs and private tutoring.

credentials

Bachelor's Degree, University of Wisconsin, 1990
Major: Computer Science
Minor: English

employers

Owner
Technical Education Inc.
5/98 to Present

Develop and present corporate training seminars. Offer individual tutoring.

Editor
Morris Educational Publishing
6/96 to 5/98

Edited educational software and technical manuals.

Sales Associate
Trayton Computers
6/94 to 6/96

Sold computer equipment and peripherals. Conducted customer training seminars.

References Available

William R. Riley

4231 Bryce Street • Boston, MA 02139 • Billriley@xxx.com • (617) 555-4973

Summary

Experienced programmer/systems designer with background in staffing, training, recruitment, supervision.

Technical Background

COBOL, PL/1, DB2, BASIC, RPG III, C, C Plus, BAL, FileAid, Ada, CAD/CAM, PASCAL, FORTRAN

Job Skills

- Software development
- Custom software design
- Corporate training programs
- Corporate recruitment
- Advanced applications and systems programming

Employers

MJ Electronics
Senior Systems Designer
June 1997 to Present

Technical Development Inc.
Software Development Specialist
March 1995 to June 1997

Revcoe Data Corporation
Systems Engineer
April 1993 to March 1995

Credentials

A.S. Computer Technology, New England Technical Institute, 1984
B.S. Business, Boston College, 1986

Member, Association of Computer Programmers and Analysts
Member, Microcomputer Software Association

References Available

Megan Herrera

410 Kane Street
Camp Hill, AL 36850
(205) 555-9075
meganherrera@xxx.com

Goal

Systems Programmer/Analyst Position

Credentials

Knowledge of BAL, CICS, BASIC, COBOL, RPG II
B.S. Computer Science, University of Georgia, 1988
A.S. Computer Repair, Atlanta Junior College, 1986

Experience

Southern Telecommunications Inc., Camp Hill
Systems Programmer
April 1998 to Present

- Install and test telecommunications software systems

Tritech Software, Atlanta
Software Designer
May 1996 to April 1998

- Develop software for business applications

Benton Computer Service, Atlanta
Computer Technician
June 1992 to May 1996

- Troubleshoot, repaired, and maintained computers and peripherals
- Trained maintenance staff

References

Available

SARAH ANN CHRISTIANSON

427 N. Spring Street
Park Ridge, IL 60068
(708) 555-3572

Summary

Programmer/analyst with extensive experience in DB2 database administration.

Technical Skills

DB2	MVS/ESA	IBM mainframes
COBOL	MVS/OS	Lotus 1-2-3
EASYTRIEVE	OS/2	CICS
SAS	IBM PCs	FileAid
VSAM	TSO/SPF	Panvalet

Employers

Crenshaw Insurance Group
Database Administrator   3/97 to Present
• DB2 testing and production activities
• Perform recovery and security functions
• Maintain compiles, sample programs, and subroutines

DuMont Financial Advisors
Systems Analyst/Programmer   6/95 to 3/97
• Performed systems analysis and programmed projects using batch COBOL and
  CICS applications
• Converted projects in VSAM, batch COBOL, and DB2

Affiliations

Women in Computer Programming
Midwest Programmers Association

Education

B.S. Information Science
Northwestern University, 1995

References Available

STEVE MADISON

2728 Clark Street
Ann Arbor, MI 48766
(313) 555-9874
stevemadison@xxx.com

BACKGROUND

Computer programmer/analyst with extensive experience installing, testing, and maintaining financial systems.

TECHNICAL SKILLS

COBOL	DB2	MS/OS
EASYTRIEVE	IDMS	MS/DOS
BASIC	RAMIS	TSO/ISPF
Pascal	Oracle (PC)	CICS
C	FileAid	Telon
Panvalet	Roscoe	INFOPAC

APPLICATIONS

- Installation and maintenance of financial systems for general ledger, check reconciliation, inventory, and cash management systems
- Creation of program specifications
- Installation of bug-fix tapes and hand fixes
- Design and writing of interfaces from in-house systems to M&D systems
- Maintenance and development of mainframe systems

EMPLOYERS

Quinn Automotive, Ann Arbor
9/98 to Present, Programmer/Analyst

Small Business Council, Ann Arbor
9/96 to 9/98, Consultant

Best Foods, Detroit
6/94 to 9/96, Systems Analyst

LT Chemical, Detroit
6/92 to 6/94, Systems Analyst

EDUCATION

B.S. Information Technology
University of Michigan, 1990

M.I.S.
Stanford University, 1992

REFERENCES AVAILABLE

Sandy Bergman

43 N. Airway • Fort Worth, TX 76137 • (817) 555-8834
sandybergman@xxx.com

System Maintenance Specialist

Overview

More than seven years of responsibility in system maintenance and upgrade. Outstanding performance reviews throughout. Tested ability to maintain systems at peak performance.

Education

B.S. in Computer Science, University of North Texas, 1993

Professional Experience

12/97 to Present, Gainey Transportation Systems, Dallas, TX
Computer Maintenance and Operations Specialist
Duties include working in an I/O area, monitoring several PCs and printing machines. Oversee memory and software upgrade involving entire system. Select and install software.

07/95 to 12/97, Telecom Systems, Fort Worth, TX
Computer Operator
Updated all customer service ledgers including accounting, payroll, and production. Input data relating to call center inquiries and oversaw troubleshooting requests. Maintained all memory and software upgrades and made hardware recommendations.

08/93 to 07/95, Ranger Tech, Tyler, TX
Computer Operator and Data Entry Clerk
Maintained printers in I/O area, operating the 6670 and 1200 Copiers. Also maintained 3800 laser printer and Versatex machines. Entered reports and maintained databases for payroll, accounting, and production.

References Available

Mitchell Spenser

5926 N. Lewis Street • Niles, IL 60714
(708) 555-0985 • mitchellspenser@xxx.com

Goal

Systems Analysis/Programming

Credentials

Knowledge of:

COBOL	DB2	MS/OS
EASYTRIEVE	IDMS	CICS
Pascal	ROSCOE	FileAid
C Plus	Oracle	INFOPAC
BASIC	MS/DOS	C

Degree in Quantitative Science
University of Wisconsin, 1995

Employers

Brooks Investing, Chicago, IL
Programmer /Analyst   10/95 to Present
Responsible for installation and programming for financial applications. Create program specifications. Code, test, install, and maintain systems.

Wyler Medical Group, Evanston, IL
Programmer   8/93 to 10/95
Converted financial systems utilizing DB2, TELON, and EASYTRIEVE Plus.

Paradigm Software, Chicago, IL
Systems Programmer   6/90 to 8/93
Installed financial systems, maintained systems. Designed and wrote interfaces.

Creighton Company, Chicago, IL
Systems Programmer   5/89 to 6/90
Supported and developed PC and mainframe systems utilizing CICS, COBOL, and BASIC.

References Available

THOMAS GILMAN

5581 Remy Avenue
San Francisco, CA 94107
(415) 555-9746 Home
(415) 555-5911 Office
thomasgilman@xxx.com

Objective: Programmer/analyst position with opportunity to create and support wide variety of PC applications

Technical Skills:

MVS JES 3	DB2	FALCON
FileAid	IBM 3033	MVS-XA
Xedit	DOS/VSE	VSAM
COBOL II	CICS	IMS-DB
Endeavor	EMC2 Disk	JCL Utilities

Employers: Amistad Corporation
7/97 to Present
Systems Analyst

San Francisco Software
6/95 to 7/97
Systems Programmer/Analyst

Paragon Printers
5/93 to 6/95
Systems Engineer

Achievements:
- Created customer profile database
- Created online credit approval system
- Revised online inventory reorder system
- Completed quality control training
- Received Amistad Employee Appreciation Award

Education: B.S. Computer Science
Stanford University

References: *Personal and professional references available*

Caroline West

2602 Riverside Drive #210
Boston, MA 02116
(617) 555-5203
carolinewest@xxx.com

Background

Systems Programmer/Analyst with experience in developing and maintaining financial systems, and an interest in acquiring software design skills.

Expertise

OS2, DB2, CICS, COBOL II, FileAid, OS/MVS, MS/DOS, INFOPAC, Data Ease, VSAM TSO/ISPF, TELON

Experience

- Developed mainframe programs
- Converted data entry system from Honeywell platform to IBM
- Developed front-end processor to reformat billing information into customer profiles using multiple IMS databases
- Performed as project manager for inventory control project group

Employers

Barton Insurance 6/97 to Present

Dayton Manufacturing 6/95 to 6/97

Education

B.S. Computer Science, University of Maine, 1995

References Available

Lydia Murray

874 Madison Street
Menlo Park, California 94025
(415) 555-3273
Cell: (415) 555-2311
lydiamurray@xxx.com

Skills

Document translation
Data processing
Database management
Software reconfiguration
Systems conversion

Technical Knowledge

COBOL, Pascal, BASIC, RPG II, FORTRAN, Lotus 1-2-3, C, C Plus,
JAVA, ASSEMBLY, ORACLE, UNIX

Employment

Data Manager, MTK Translation Service, 9/97 to Present
Systems Analyst, Ashworth Corporation, 8/95 to 9/97

Education

B.S., University of California, Davis
Computer Science/Mathematics

Member, Association of Computer Professionals

REFERENCES AVAILABLE

ROBERT A. STEIN
5523 Gallery Drive
Hasbrouck Heights, NJ 07606
(201) 555-3213
robertstein@xxx.com

Goal: Computer Engineering

Technical Skills: UNIX   BASIC   VSAM
                        C   AutoCAD   MS/DOS
                        Pascal   FileAid   CICS
                        FORTRAN   COBOL   MVS-XA

Education: M.I.S. Cornell University

                        B.S. Syracuse University

Job Skills: Development of software specifications
                        Custom software design
                        Product support
                        Project management
                        Systems programming
                        Systems conversion projects

Employers: Saxton Software Inc.
                        Software Engineer
                        11/97 to Present

                        IDP Manufacturing
                        Project Manager
                        10/95 to 11/97

                        First Savings and Loan of Hasbrouck Heights
                        Systems Programmer
                        5/92 to 10/95

References: Available on request

Kevin Dugan

8641 Palama Road
Midlothian, Virginia 23113
804-555-8265
kevdugan@xxx.com

Background

Experienced computer consultant specializing in long-term corporate consulting/training projects.

Credentials

Knowledge of BASIC, C Plus, MS/DOS, COBOL, Pascal, FORTRAN, DOS/VSE, ASSEMBLY, UNIX

B.S. Computer Science, William and Mary College, 1994

Clients

AT DUNHILL CORPORATION: *Ongoing*
- Technical Support, including equipment selection and supervision of installation
- Custom software design
- Employee training seminars

CORRIGAN DESIGN INC.: *Six-Month Project*
- Implementation of new quality control procedures
- Employee training sessions

UNIVERSITY OF VIRGINIA: *Eight-Month Project*
- Creation and installation of schema and subsystem flow for general ledger system.
- Development of PC hardware and software standards.

Business and personal references available on request.

Julie Prescott

372 Burroughs Street • Cleveland, OH 44138 • (216) 555-5145 • juliep@xxx.com

Background

Technical supervisor with specialization in data processing, familiar with UNISYS equipment and CICS systems programming.

Expertise

DOS/VSE	IMS	EASYTRIEVE
CICS	NCP	COBOL
DL1	VTAM	Assembler
MS/DOS	BASIC	Pascal
XEDIT	DEC-10	DBASE II

Employment

Bradley Manufacturing
Data Processing Supervisor 7/98 to Present

Direct start-up of new data control center, including installation of all workstations and peripheral equipment. Establish data control procedures. Assist in hiring and training new staff.

Star Data Corporation
Database Manager 4/96 to 7/98

Managed data processing department, including all data entry and output, using UNISYS equipment. Supervised staff of eight.

APT Chemical Corporation
Data Control Specialist   6/94 to 4/96

Responsible for maintenance of 150-terminal network. Supported online batch order-processing function.

Education

B.S. Information Technology
Ohio State University, 1994

References

Corey Smith	Mary Blodgett
Vice President, Finance	Data Processing Manager
Bradley Manufacturing	Star Data Corporation
(216) 555-6204	(216) 555-7806

Jay Maher

•

877 N. Misano Dr.
Virginia Beach, VA 23456
(804) 555-1223
jaymaher@xxx.com

Web Master

Triplesearch.com
Developed, from scratch, fully interactive website devoted to streamlining Web-based researching. Integrated databases of three major university research departments into one easily navigated site. Wrote all coding for site including Java, Flash, and HTML. Employed Adobe Photoshop to manipulate photos and create eye-catching banner ads. Also tested and debugged entire 375-page site to ensure all links and functionality worked.

Songswap.com
Created and promoted peer-to-peer file sharing website featured in several national magazines including *Time* magazine, *Rolling Stone,* and *Spin.* Generated hits exceeding 100,000 a day. Upgraded system several times to handle site traffic and eventually integrated system into another commercial site upon its sale.

Theword.com
Online gossip magazine twice awarded "Webbies" and one of the first to attain 3W compliance. Received several national awards for design and functionality and often cited as a pioneering site in the early development of the web.

The Web is my passion and despite recent downturns in the tech industry, it remains a formidable force. The proper construction and promotion of a website can introduce a company to millions of perspective customers in the blink of an eye. I can help develop that site. I've already proven it.

Screen shots and press clippings available

michael tomasa
programmer/analyst

677 Gardner Road   (610) 555-5722 Office
Morton, PA 19070   (610) 555-6773 Home

skills   Knowledge of COBOL, DEC VAX 11/780, ASIC, C,
                    FORTRAN, NATURAL, Pascal
                    Familiar with IBM, Compaq, and Apple PCs

education   B.S. Computer science
                    University of Virginia, 1996

employers   V-Tech Software Systems
                    Senior Systems Analyst
                    4/99 to Present

                    Quest Processors Inc.
                    Systems Analyst/Programmer
                    3/97 to 4/99

                    M&R Business support
                    MIS Technician
                    2/96 to 3/97

assignments   Custom software design

                    Product support for software line

                    Technical support for end users

references   On request

Tracy Bahls

742 Lindsey Lane • East Greenwich, RI 02818 • 401-555-7319

Goal

Software Engineering Position

Credentials

M.I.S.   Rhode Island Technical Institute
B.S.   Queens College

DEC VAX 11/780, Intel Software, C,
Unix Systems, MS/DOS, VMS, Pascal, BASIC, Macro II

Experience

Princeton Computer Supplies   **9/98 to Present**
Senior Systems Designer

Develop I/0 interfaces and create/support file transfer
systems. Extensive use of Intel software and DEC VAX
11/780 in C Language

Superior Software   **6/96 to 9/98**
Technical Advisor

Marketing and sales support for extensive software
products line including spreadsheets, word processing
programs, graphics, and database applications.

Little Young Development   **5/91 to 6/96**
Team leader for software development projects.

Promoted after one year from programmer to senior
programmer.

References

Available

Gary Johnson

2513 Corbett Street
Charleston, WV 25304
(304) 555-2815
garyjohnson@xxx.com

GOAL

Applications/Systems Programming

SKILLS

COBOL	FORTRAN	Pascal
C	C Plus	BASIC
RPG II	EASYTRIEVE	CAD/CAM
CICS	ANS	VSAM

EDUCATION

B.S. Computer Science
University of Georgia, 1995

EMPLOYERS

Lincoln Investing	Webster Software Inc.
Systems Programmer	Applications Programmer
4/97 to Present	6/95 to 4/97

Duties:
- Create program specifications and documentation
- Review and select hardware and software packages
- Modify software packages for compatibility with existing systems
- Code, test, debug, and maintain systems
- Respond to systems error messages
- Maintain database packages, compilers, assemblers, and utility programs

REFERENCES

Personal and professional references are available

William Rothman

642 Oak Street
Chicago, IL 60645
(312) 555-4905
billrothman@xxx.com

Objective

Technical Writing

Technical Expertise

COBOL	IFPS	TELON
DB2	EASYTRIEVE	CICS
ROSCOE	BASIC	Pascal

Experience

- Preparation and revision of reference manuals for end users based on technical information and specifications gathered from programmers and systems engineers.
- Customer service for end users, supporting both hardware and software.
- Maintenance of phone log recording customer problems for use in modification of systems designs and revision of technical manuals.

Employers

3/99 to Present
Technical Writer
Lexus Software Products, Evanston, IL

2/95 to 3/99
Customer Service Technician
Sullivan Software Inc., Chicago, IL

Education

B.S. Computer Technology
Southern Illinois University, 1989

References Available

MELISSA WRIGHT

2132 Alcott Street • Cleveland, Ohio 44138
(216) 555-4613
missywright@xxx.com

EXPERIENCE

First National Bank of Cleveland
Data Processing Manager
September 1997 to Present

Manage department of six data processors responsible for all data processing in support of financial systems. Prioritize, assign, and coordinate projects. Staff, evaluate, and schedule department.

Talon Computing Equipment Inc.
Computer Operator
June 1994 to September 1997

Operated computer system utilized for inventory control, purchasing, customer recordkeeping, and general ledger functions.

Chevron Manufacturing
Inventory Control Clerk
April 1992 to June 1994

Responsible for data entry, inventory control, order tracking, and creation of status reports.

EDUCATION

University of South Florida, St. Petersburg
B.A. in Business Administration, 1992
Coursework in COBOL, PL/1, RPG III, and C

AFFILIATIONS

Member, Data Processing Management Association

Member, Women in Data Processing

REFERENCES

Anita Walker   Michael Weiss
Human Resources Director   Data Control Manager
First National Bank of Cleveland   Chevron Manufacturing
(216) 555-6200, ext. 122   (216) SSS-7246
anitawalker@xxx.com   mikeweiss@xxx.com

Charles Rangoon

2397 N. Ridgeview Ln.
Brookfield, WI 53045
(414) 555-2334
charlesrangoon@xxx.com

Professional Objective

Computer programmer position with opportunities for challenges and advancement

Summary

- B.S. in Computer and Information Sciences
- Specific expertise in FORTRAN, COBOL, Pascal, C, and Basic
- Programming experience using VAX/VMS
- Outstanding performance reviews from past and present employers

Employment History

1997 to Present - Ansill Electronics, Brookfield, WI
Heavy coding using PLI and COBOL with emphasis on program structure,
language efficiency, and maintainability. Assisted project leader in defining and
resolving application project malfunctions and failures.

1995 to 1997 - Smith Industries, Brookfield, WI
Responsibilities included user contact, developing user specifications, program
design, coding, debugging, and support. Coding primarily done in FORTRAN/77
under VM/CMS on IBM 370.

References

Karen White, Ansill Electronics
Supervisor
(414) 555-6632

Robert Standell, Ansill Electronics
President
(414) 555-8993

Judy Smith, Smith Industries
President
(414) 555-3345

MARGOT SAYRES

482 Wentworth Street
Chicago, IL 60046
(312) 555-0181
margot35@xxx.com

SUMMARY

- Engineering and programming experience
- Strong organizational and communications skills
- Excellent record of meeting deadlines
- Cost effective solutions to complex programming and design challenges

EDUCATION

Bachelor's Degree, Computer Science
Western Illinois University, 1994

Master's Degree, Electrical Engineering
University of Illinois, Champaign, 1996

Coursework in BASIC, C, Pascal, FORTRAN, COBOL, VSAM, CICS, and
Unix

EMPLOYERS

IDS International
Senior Engineer   1998 to Present

Implement automatic assembly systems for manufacturer of computer peripherals. Design, test, and support process-control programs.

DataTel Communications
Applications Programmer   1997 to 1998

Planned and developed data products. Created individualized applications for
clients, including integration of voice and data over PBX by linking PCs and
peripherals in a Network.

Central Data Corporation
Technical Programmer   1994 to 1997

Managed data processing department. Responsible for systems programming
in Assembler for Univac 9300 system.

References Available

Jonathan Brimwell

8845 N. Kenewa Dr.
Sun City, AZ 85351

(602) 555-3221
(602) 555-2399
jonathan@xxx.com

Education

B.S. Computer Science
University of Arizona, 1994

Relevant Studies

BAL	FORTRAN	PASCAL
LISP	SNOBOL	COBOL
C	C Plus	UNIX
dbase	BASIC	

Professional Experience

Programmer, Gardner Inc.
9/99 to present
Design, write, and implement business software systems using appropriate databases. Integrate database packages and operating systems. Recommend appropriate software and hardware upgrades. Maintain PCs and train new personnel.

Programmer/Analyst, DirectQuest Systems
5/97 to 9/99
Designed, coded, and implemented online batch functions. Wrote residual program maintenance, product type maintenance, residual AE purge, and benefit reporting. Programmed in COBOL and CICS COMMAND LEVEL.

Programmer, InSTALL, Inc.
6/94 to 5/97
Duties included debugging, documentation, data validation, and problem analysis on software used by telemarketing team. Redesigned and documented interactive programs resulting in 20 percent increase in productivity.

References available

Andrew Branson

4556 N. Claremont • Grand Rapids, MI 49503
(616) 555-9987 • andybranson@xxx.com

Goal

Find a position as a Programmer Analyst in which I can apply my extensive knowledge of software and hardware.

Experience

Several years working with COBOL, CICS/VS, and command level VSAM files.

Technical Ability

CICS, ANS Cobol, VSAM, OS/JCL, OS/MVS, and TSO/SPF

Work History

6/97 to present
Senior Programmer Analyst
Autodie, Inc., Grand Rapids, MI

Design and implement inventory trading system. All programs run in CICS/VSAM environment. Inventory control has improved more than 35 percent since implementation.

9/95 to 6/97
Consultant
Gilmore Bank, Kalamazoo, MI

Oversaw ATM ministatement project. Developed the interface between Host and Tandem subsystem to retrieve last ten transactions via ISC and LU 3270 environment.

12/89 to 9/95
Programmer Analyst
StarTech, Inc., Flint, MI

Responsibilities included: running batch jobs to convert IMS files to DB2 table format; maintenance of DB2 batch/online programs using APS macros; and optimizing performance on application programs.

References

Alan Andrews	Shana Wilson	Lucida Perez
Vice President of Production	Systems Manager	233 N. Lamont, Ste. 1134
Autodie, Inc.	Gilmore Bank	Flint, MI 48503
4656 Oak St.	7733 N. Wilmott	(517) 555-3344
Grand Rapids, MI 49544	Kalamazoo, MI 49006	lucidaperez@xxx.com
(616) 555-8334	(616) 555-9554	
alanandrews@xxx.com	shanaw@xxx.com	

Juan Cordoba

234 N. Star Lane • Boise, ID 83706
Home (208) 555-4332 • Cell (208) 555-2266
Juancordoba@xxx.com

System Consultant

Specialties

Computer Networks
Local Area Networks
Computer Engineering
Communications Systems
Digital Signal Processing
Digital Electronics

Specific Skills

Fortran
Assembly
PASCAL
CICS
BASIC
COBOL

Employment

Axiom Systems Inc. (10/99 to Present)
Systems Consultant
Consulting work on IBM PC, PC/XT, PC/AT, PC/RT, System 36/PC, Novell Network. Coordinate software upgrades and database backups. Troubleshoot network problems and outages.

Continental Cable Systems (05/95 to 10/99)
System Analyst
Monitored LAN and maintained operation. Ensured computer networks were updated and logs were current. Supervised a staff of 10 analysts and programmers. Delegated work, administered evaluations, and oversaw professional development.

Beltway Business Solutions
Programmer/Analyst
Consulted with companies to develop Local Area Networks and communications networks. Worked closely with clients to establish their needs and capabilities and then formulated realistic recommendations.

References

Max Stout
VP Networking
Axiom Systems Inc.
(208) 555-8823
maxstout@xxx.com

Julie Detmiller
Manager
Continental Cable Systems
(208) 555-1230
juliedetmiller@xxx.com

Ben Benedict
President
Beltway Business Solutions
(208) 555-7694
benbenedict@xxx.com

Additional References Available

• *Cindy Cannon* •

3344 N. Western Ave.
Chicago, IL 60625
773-555-1998
cindycannon@xxx.com

Data Analyst

•

• *Summary*

Exceptional organizational skills. Over seven years business experience in a variety of settings. Proven ability to utilize extensive knowledge of information systems.

• *Employment*

Programmer Analyst
Midcom Legal Consultation, Chicago, IL   9/96 to present

Responsible for support of an integrated legal practice system, which includes subsystems for rate filings and document orders from federal, state, and local government agencies. Develop project standards and procedures as well as train others.

Programmer Analyst
InterDesign, Inc., Evanston, IL   6/94 to 9/96

Oversaw maintenance of batch and online systems. Trained and supervised junior employees using DPPX/DSX programs. Analyzed business systems to identify conversion, interface, and technical requirements. Redesigned company mailing system.

• *Technical Knowledge*

IBM 3090 and 4381, PS/2, Windows, DB2, TSO/ISPF, QMF, MVS-ESA, CICS, VSAM, and Pascal.

References available at your request

Chapter 6

Sample Cover Letters

This chapter contains many sample cover letters for people pursuing a wide variety of jobs and careers in the field of computers, or who have had experience in this field in the past.

There are many different styles of cover letters in terms of layout, level of formality, and presentation of information. These samples also represent people with varying amounts of education and work experience. Choose one cover letter or borrow elements from several different cover letters to help you construct your own.

May 28, 20--

Derek J. Van
Director of Networked Operations
Van Enterprises
1234 Rockefeller Drive
Los Angeles, California 91108

Dear Mr. Van:

Susan Scharf, of CompuScan Corporation, recommended that I contact you about professional opportunities that might exist within your company.

For the past six years I have been working in the area of software development for a major software company here in Los Angeles. In that time, I have worked independently and on teams to develop a number of highly successful software programs for use at home and in offices.

Although I enjoy my work, I am ready to move on to new products and a new company. I have been particularly impressed with your products over the past few years, especially those focusing on networking applications for both large- and small-scale commercial operations.

I would welcome the opportunity to speak with you about Van Enterprises and the ways in which I could make a valuable contribution to your team and your bottom line. I have attached my resume for your consideration and will call in a week or so to see about coming in and discussing my qualifications in person.

I look forward to speaking with you.

Sincerely,

Estrella Magana
1299 Old Mill Road
San Marino, CA 91023

CATHY SMITH
546 Elm Street
Chicago, IL 60645

June 11, 20--

Mr. Paul T. West
Director of Customer Service
Technoserve Inc.
132 E. Pearson Street
Wauconda, IL 60084

Dear Mr. West:

I enjoyed our conversation this morning regarding the customer service department at Technoserve, and I am looking forward to my interview next Tuesday. Technoserve has an excellent reputation in the software industry, and I would be pleased to be associated with your firm. I also feel confident that my experience as a customer service professional and a technical writer would allow me to make a significant contribution to your department.

As the enclosed resume explains, I have worked in the field for more than 12 years and enjoy the challenges of technical writing and customer service. In my current position at Superior Software Products, I create technical manuals for Superior's software line, which includes desktop publishing, graphic arts, word processing, and database products. My supervisor has praised my ability to translate technical information into clear instructions for end users.

My previous position, at Worthington Software, gave me customer service experience. As a customer service technician, I took great pride in being able to troubleshoot for our clients and guide them in the step-by-step solution of their online difficulties. I would enjoy being able to assist Technoserve's customers in the same way.

If any questions arise before next Tuesday, I am most easily reached before noon at my home number: 312-555-3894. I appreciate the opportunity to meet with you to discuss putting my skills to work for Technoserve.

Sincerely,

Cathy Smith

Martin K. Meade
411 West Street • Boston, MA 02129

May 16, 20--

Ms. Robin Haight
Human Resources Manager
Lombard Business Machines Inc.
8700 Mission Street
Boston, MA 02129

Dear Ms. Haight:

I wish to apply for the Senior Systems Analyst position you advertised this week in the *Boston Globe*. The enclosed resume outlines my background in programming and systems analysis.

Your ad indicated that you require an experienced systems analyst with knowledge of CICS, DB2, and COBOL. I meet these requirements and would be pleased to tackle the professional challenge of serving as your new Senior Systems Analyst.

May I present my credentials in person? You may reach me at 555-5600 from 8 A.M. to 4 P.M., or at 555-6786 after 4 P.M., to arrange an interview.

Yours truly,

Martin K. Meade

BARBARA ZABRISKIE
655 COOK ROAD
ORMOND BEACH, FL 32176

April 5, 20--

Mr. Warren Baker
Human Resources Director
Wilson & Smythe Data Management Inc.
902 E. Parker Drive
Ormond Beach, FL 32176

Dear Mr. Baker:

A colleague of mine, Julia Ortega, suggested that I write to you regarding independent contracting opportunities at Wilson & Smythe. I work with Julia at Warren Manufacturing where I am currently a senior programmer. Although I enjoy my present job, I am interested in taking on the challenge of becoming an independent contractor. Perhaps Wilson & Smythe can become one of my first clients.

Are you interested in a talented programmer/systems analyst with proven skills in data processing? Do you require DB2 and CICS analysis, design, and development? If so, my resume should interest you. My previous experience includes development, specifications writing, logical and physical design, structural procedures testing, and various financial applications using COBOL, DB2, CICS, and VSAM.

I am available at your convenience if you would like to arrange an interview. You may reach me at work, 555-2078, from 9 A.M. to 5 P.M. My home number is 555-4968.

Thank you for considering how I might be of assistance to Wilson & Smythe.

Sincerely,

Barbara Zabriskie

Beverly Jackson
1800 West Sheridan Avenue
Atlanta, Georgia 30356

November 27, 20--

Mr. Michael Walker
Data Processing Coordinator
Tallac Technical Services
2201 Stearns Road
Atlanta, Georgia 30356

Dear Mr. Walker:

I was pleased to hear that you are in the market for a programming consultant. I have always been interested in working at Tallac and would like to apply for the position.

My experience as an independent programmer has given me a wide range of technical skills, the details of which are listed on the enclosed resume. I am confident that many of these skills are the same ones you currently require:

• Specifications Writing
• Design and Coding of New Programs
• Structural Procedure Testing
• Program Modifications

I appreciate your taking time to review my credentials. I will call next week to arrange an interview so that we can discuss how I might put my skills to work for Tallac Technical.

Cordially,

Beverly Jackson
(707) 555-4580

RP On-Line Inc.

372 Ashurst Road
Boulder, CO 80321
(303) 555-5121

September 12, 20--

Ah Hing Choy
Senior Systems Analyst
Thatcher Bearing Company Ltd.
4890 Summers Road
Boulder, CO 80321

Dear Mr. Choy:

Your recent ad in *Computer Design* for a Program Designer attracted my attention because your current needs match my programming and design skills exactly. I have managed my own consulting firm for the past ten years but am willing to work in-house if the right opportunity presents itself.

The enclosed resume explains my credentials in some detail. Please let me know if you need further information to evaluate my qualifications. You can reach me from 8 A.M. to 4 P.M. at 303-555-5121. I am also available at your convenience if you would like to meet with me.

I look forward to hearing how I might contribute to the success of Thatcher Bearing.

Sincerely,

Randy Paterniti
Owner, R.P. On-Line Inc.

Deborah S. Drew
President
Drew Enterprises
56 Gabriel Street
Wichita, Kansas 67219

March 11, 20--

Dear Ms. Drew:

I am an independent consultant with a twenty-year record of producing quality work. Clients value my skill, dedication, and respect for deadlines. They appreciate being able to confidently delegate programming and systems analysis projects to me.

Is your organization currently in need of technical support? If so, I would appreciate hearing from you. I am available during the day at 708-555-5732, and I have enclosed a resume for your review.

Please let me know if I may assist you.

Sincerely,

Kevin Schultz
1302 Willow Road
Oak Brook, IL 60521

Nancy Guerrero
Personnel Director
HDS Medical
911 Griffin Street
Cottonwood, CA 96022

May 22, 20--

Dear Ms. Guerrero:

I submit the enclosed resume in the hope that you may be in need of someone with my technical background. Please note that I have been a successful computer consultant for the past ten years. It has been my privilege to serve a wide variety of clients during that time, and I would bring a wealth of experience to HDS Medical.

I am currently finishing a project for the Wakefield Architectural Group and will be available for assignments again in mid-June. My supervisor at Wakefield, Paul Martin, is pleased with my performance and has agreed to act as a reference. You may contact him at (916) 555-5867, ext. 327.

If you need to speak to me, I am most easily reached at home at (916) 555-6333 after 3 P.M.

Thank you for your consideration. I look forward to your reply.

Sincerely,

Davis P. Robinson

Karen Feldman
877 Chesterfield Street • Lincolnwood, IL 60646 • (708) 555-9113
Cell: (708) 555-7768 • karenfeldman@xxx.com

March 16, 20--

Mr. William Howell
Senior Programmer
ADC Information Systems
490 Gregory Road
Lincolnwood, IL 60646

Dear Bill:

As I mentioned when we spoke last week, I will soon be available for new projects. My current assignment at New Age Organic Foods will be completed by the end of the month. I've been working for a former colleague of yours, Phil Preston, and have enjoyed the assignment very much.

I'm glad to hear that you may have a need for my skill set in the near future. Please call as projects develop. I would welcome the opportunity to work for you again.

Sincerely,

Karen Feldman

TO: Evelyn Yashiro
           Human Resources Manager
           Advantage Insurance Inc.
           5622 Winston Circle
           Des Moines, IA 50309

DATE: February 12, 20--

RE: Technical Writing Position

Translating technical material into clear, concise English is a skill that all corporations value. Advantage Insurance is no exception, as your recent ad for technical writers indicates. I feel confident that I could meet your high standards, and I would welcome the challenge of creating documentation for your computer department.

My qualifications for the position are explained in detail in the enclosed resume. The highlights are as follows:

- Successful creation of online manuals, standards, and systems documentation for current and previous employers.
- Six years' technical writing experience in corporate environments.
- B.A. from University of Iowa with background in both liberal arts and computer science.

Please let me know if I can supply any other information that will assist you as you evaluate my credentials. I look forward to hearing how I might add to the continued success of your organization.

Cordially,

Howard L. Meyers
1394 Freeland Road
Des Moines, IA 50309-3023
(515) 555-4421, from 8 A.M. to 4 P.M.
(515) 555-1143, after 4 P.M.
howardmeyers@xxx.com

Maria Frederick

902 Hills Street
Stanford, CA 94305
(415) 555-7194
mariafrederick@xxx.com

June 16, 20--

Kevin Denziger, Senior Systems Designer
Syntech Inc.
47 W. Park Street
San Francisco, CA 94105

Dear Mr. Denziger:

Your ad in this month's *Software* magazine caught my eye. I am enclosing my resume and a list of references so that you may consider me for the systems programming position.

I have been a systems programmer for nearly a decade, as the enclosed resume explains. My experience includes software development, testing, and modification, plus systems design and maintenance. Please note the aspects of my professional background that qualify me for the position:

- Extensive systems design experience through my positions at Creative Technologies and DataPro Corporation.
- Strong writing skills developed while creating manuals and development tools for both corporations.
- Effective teaching skills developed as data processing instructor at DataPro.

I am confident that my skills would enhance the operation of Syntech Inc., and I look forward to speaking with you in person.

Thanks for your consideration.

Sincerely,

Maria Frederick

Barbara Danbury

9950 Brockport Road • Houston, Texas 77386 • Barbaradanbury@xxx.com

Bennet Smith, Director
Technical Personnel
411 Clark Street
Houston, Texas 77386

May 19, 19--

Dear Mr. Smith:

Like many other programmers, my long-term career goal is to own a consulting business. I know that to achieve that goal I need to acquire the most diverse background possible. Working for Technical Personnel would give me that opportunity. Several of your current employees, including Renee Stine and Paul Muir, have told me of their positive experiences working for you.

What can I add to Technical Personnel? I am an experienced programmer whose background includes program design, testing, and documentation. The enclosed resume provides details, and both Ms. Stine and Mr. Muir are familiar with my work should you need a reference.

Thanks for taking time to consider my qualifications. I look forward to the possibility of joining the staff of fine programmers at Technical Personnel.

Sincerely,

Barbara Danbury
(713) 555-0194 Home
(713) 555-8690 Office
barbaradanbury@xxx.com

TO: Joe Poole
               Senior Systems Designer
               Wexler Dante Inc.
               7757 Gulch Road
               Amherst, NH 03031

FROM: Ray Pierce
               3102 Hopper Street
               Cambridge, MA 02139
               (617) 555-3862

DATE: June 15, 20--

RE: Application for Systems Designer Position

I enjoyed talking to you this morning about the custom software you design at Wexler Dante. Wexler Dante has an impressive client list, and I'm sure it will continue to grow as your department expands.

It pleased me to hear that you may have room for me on your staff. I have enclosed my resume, which explains in detail my work experience. If you have other questions before we meet on the 24th, you can reach me at 617-555-3862.

Two former supervisors have agreed to provide references for me. The first is Dawn Basco, senior programmer at Triton; her number is 617-555-2162. The second is Jason Hasset, General Manager of Technical Data Corporation. Jason's number is 617-555-1200, ext. 522.

Thanks for your interest. I look forward to talking with you on the 24th.

Ms. Heidi Dawson
Human Resources Director
Thornton Software Inc.
314 S. Hatcher Lane
Savannah, GA 31498

July 9, 20--

Dear Ms. Dawson:

As an experienced systems programmer with a strong interest in robotics, I think I could make a unique contribution to Thornton Software. Please take a moment to review the enclosed resume, which explains my professional background.

I am fortunate to have had a wide variety of programming and design assignments. In addition, I have teaching and computer maintenance and repair skills. This varied background would serve me well in designing software for Thornton.

I would appreciate hearing of any opening for which I qualify, and I am available at your convenience if you wish to interview me.

Thank you for your consideration.

Sincerely,

Martha Smith
307 Afton Road
Camp Hill, AL 368SO
(205) 555-8964
marthasmith@xxx.com

JEAN A. JENKINS

216 S. Fulton Street • Park Ridge, IL 60068
708-555-2461 • jeanjenkins@xxx.com

May 21, 20--

Ms. Barbara King
Personnel Director
Wellington Corporation
7675 Arbor Lane
Des Plaines, IL 60018

Dear Ms. King:

The position you recently advertised in the *Chicago Tribune* seems to match my skills exactly. As the senior database administrator at Munroe Insurance, I support all DB2 testing and production activities. The programming skills I have mastered at Munroe would translate well to the database administration position you are seeking to fill.

The enclosed resume provides the details of my professional accomplishments. My salary requirements are negotiable.

I will contact you next week to arrange an interview. Meanwhile, thank you for your consideration.

Sincerely,

Jean A. Jenkins

Patrick C. Carter

1617 Emory Street

Forsyth, GA 31029

(912) 555-4612

Patcarter@xxx.com

July 13, 20--

Mr. Edward Goldman
Senior Analyst
Atlanta Manufacturing Inc.
108 Trenton Road
Atlanta, GA 30301

Dear Mr. Goldman:

I enjoyed meeting you last week at the Computer Technology Show. Your firm's use of robotics interests me, and I would appreciate having a chance to talk to you further regarding programming positions at Atlanta Manufacturing.

As you know, I am a programmer/analyst at RTP Chemical. I have also worked for two Atlanta firms: Taylor Business Group and Lee & Jacobsen Manufacturing. The enclosed resume provides the details of my work history.

I will call early next week to discuss opportunities at Atlanta Manufacturing.

Sincerely,

Patrick C. Carter

CORBIN DREYFUS
7530 Cypress Street • Midlothian, VA 23113

September 6, 20--

Ms. Shelley Strauss, Director
Technical Recruitment Inc.
418 Heritage Road
Richmond, VA 23298

Dear Ms. Strauss:

Thank you for calling to inquire about my interest in corporate training assignments. Enclosed is the resume you requested. As you can see, I frequently work with corporations who are installing or upgrading micro- or mainframe computer systems.

In addition to the technical skills listed on my resume, I have a strong work ethic, an excellent record of meeting deadlines, and proven teaching ability. I feel confident that your clients would value these qualities, as have my former employers.

If you need further information or would like to schedule an interview, I am available most mornings at 804-555-7154.

Thank you for your interest.

Sincerely,

Corbin Dreyfus

Attn: Ken Shapiro
Nova Software Systems
804 S. Ferris Street
Falls Church, Virginia 22042

May 19, 20--

Dear Mr. Shapiro:

Is your firm in need of a talented professional with software design, support, and marketing experience? Someone who shares your commitment to innovative programming? If so, my resume should interest you. I am a successful software/systems engineer in search of new professional challenges.

My background includes knowledge of Unix, C, Pascal, FORTRAN, BASIC, VSAM, CICS, and AutoCAD. If you feel my skills match your current needs, please call me at 201-555-2102.

Thanks for your consideration.

Sincerely,

Daniel Threlkeld
4412 Trask Road
Hasbrouck Heights, NJ 07606
Danthrekeld@xxx.com

Jill Eisenberg

261 Merrill Street • Cleveland, Ohio 44138
(216) 555-4034 • jilly@xxx.com

October 10, 20--

Ms. Edith Miller
Human Resources Director
Superior Foods
129 Walton Street
Cleveland, OH 44138

Dear Ms. Miller:

Efficient data processing is crucial to the operation of any organization. My application for the position of Data Processing Manager comes with the assurance that I understand the pivotal role that information management plays in your firm's success.

I am an experienced technical services supervisor familiar with UNISYS equipment, NCP/VTAM and CICS systems programming, as well as mainframe/transactions database environments. My resume, which is enclosed, provides further details.

If you feet my qualifications warrant serious consideration, you may reach me at 216-555-4034.

Cordially,

Jill Eisenberg

Mr. David Mitchell
Computronics Inc.
9355 Covington Circle
Richardson, TX 75083

May 14, 20--

Dear Mr. Mitchell:

Your ad in *Database Programming and Design* has prompted me to contact you. I have experience designing software for business applications. In my current position with Corporate Software Inc., I have been working on invoice and order processing applications in COBOL using DEC VAX 11/780 hardware. These skills are quite similar to those you now require.

Please take a moment to review the enclosed resume. I am sure you will agree that my background in software design makes me an excellent candidate for the position of Senior Programmer.

I am willing to relocate for the right position, and my salary requirements are negotiable.

I appreciate your consideration of my credentials and look forward to hearing more about programming opportunities at Computronics.

Sincerely,

Michelle Tyler
3116 Ventura Street
Morton, PA 19070
(610) 555-4611

October 26, 20--

Joshua Rogers
3445 Park St.
New York, NY 10177
(212) 555-2776
joshuarogers@xxx.com

Ms. Amanda Jackson
Director of Human Resources
Charlotte Digital Systems, Inc.
145 Park Ave.
New York, NY 10172

Dear Ms. Jackson,

I am interested in the programming position you have available. As you can
see from my resume, I have almost ten years of experience in programming
for a variety of platforms. My background spans a wide range of industries
and I believe this diverse background makes me an excellent candidate for
this position.

I have a history of dedication to job and enthusiasm. My past employers will
tell you I am a thoughtful, thorough programmer who always looks for the
details, asks questions, and delivers dependable programs. Please contact
my references and see for yourself what kind of reputation I've built for
myself.

I am available for personal interviews at your convenience and look forward
to hearing from you soon.

Sincerely,

Joshua Rogers

Michael DeRuiter

2349 N. Bosworth • Bradenton, FL 34203
(941) 555-5556
mikederuiter@xxx.com

September 22, 20--

Alan Genter, President
MonoTech
Tampa, FL 34212

Mr. Genter:

I am writing in regards to the Web design position you have posted on your website. Upon review of my work, I think you'll agree that I have designed some of the most startling and appealing sites on the Web today. I strive to draw in visitors to the sites I design to a full experience. With the millions of options out there, a company is always a click away from losing a perspective customer. My designs coupled with your company's unique product offering ensures that MonoTech can succeed in this highly competitive industry.

I would like to meet personally to show you some of the full-color comps I have of previous sites I've designed and to also walk you through some of the sites that are live and successful on the Web using my carefully thought out and executed concepts.

Please feel free to call me any time to discuss my qualifications and your expectations. I look forward to our conversation.

Sincerely,

Mike DeRuiter

Kim Lee

87 Cove Road
Lake Wylie, NC 29710
(794) 555-5133
kimlee@xxx.com

John Maxson
Independiente, LLC
Charlotte, NC 29712

Dear Sir:

Joyce Sellers, Senior Programmer, Independiente, LLC, told me of
a programming position you may soon have available. Joyce and I
worked together for six years at Huxom Industries as programmers
and she is well aware of the quality of work I deliver. My experience
as a programmer of complex database systems, LAN, and Internal
Networks has given me the kind of background that can be of great
assistance to you and your company.

My current position demands that I ensure all networks are working
smoothly and that all upgrades are completed in a timely manner.
While I have enjoyed my time here at Huxom, I am now ready for a
greater challenge and I believe that challenge lies in Independiente,
LLC.

Please feel free to discuss my background and skills with Joyce. I also
have other references available at your request. I hope to hear from
you soon and I thank you for your time.

Sincerely,

Kim Lee